Python AI Programming

Navigating fundamentals of ML, deep learning, NLP, and reinforcement learning in practice

Patrick J

GitforGits™
ASIAN PUBLISHING HOUSE

Published by: GitforGits
Publisher: Sonal Dhandre
www.gitforgits.com
support@gitforgits.com

Printed in India

First Printing: January 2024

ISBN: 978-8119177639

Cover Design by: Kitten Publishing

Prologue

Welcome to "Python AI Programming," an opening into the transformational world of Artificial Intelligence as seen through the prism of Python, the language that has come to be synonymous with modern AI development. This book was written with the goal of taking you, the aspiring AI developer, on an illuminating trip through the fundamental aspects of AI, all articulated in the versatile and intuitive language of Python.

Our adventure starts with a detailed overview of Python's principles, revealing how this language is the ideal toolkit for aspiring AI practitioners. As we progress, the domains of Machine Learning and Deep Learning unveil themselves, illustrating how Python's libraries and frameworks are crucial in pioneering advances in these fields. Each chapter advances your AI learning curve, from the fundamentals of data management to the complexity of neural networks.

When you dive into the complexities of Natural Language Processing (NLP), you'll discover Python's strength in parsing human language, a talent that's critical in today's data-driven world. The story then takes you through the intriguing worlds of Computer Vision and Reinforcement Learning, where Python's skills shine in training machines to visually understand the world and make intelligent decisions.

However, as we welcome these technical marvels, we must be mindful of AI ethics. This book teaches you to think ethically as well as code, ensuring that the AI you design is responsible and useful to all.

Remember that this book is more than simply a technical book as you turn each page; it is a companion on your journey to becoming an AI developer. It's about understanding the 'why' as much as the 'how,' about seeing a future in which technology boosts human capacities, fueled by your newfound skills and insights.

Content

Preface

This book aspires young graduates and programmers to become AI engineers and enter the world of artificial intelligence by combining powerful Python programming with artificial intelligence. Beginning with the fundamentals of Python programming, the book gradually progresses to machine learning, where readers learn to implement Python in developing predictive models. The book provides a clear and accessible explanation of machine learning, incorporating practical examples and exercises that strengthen understanding.

We go deep into deep learning, another vital component of AI. Readers gain a thorough understanding of how Python's frameworks and libraries can be used to create sophisticated neural networks and algorithms, which are required for tasks such as image and speech recognition. Natural Language Processing is also covered in the book, with fundamental concepts and techniques for interpreting and generating human-like language covered. The book's focus on computer vision and reinforcement learning is distinctive, presenting these cutting-edge AI fields in an approachable manner.

Readers will learn how to use Python's intuitive programming paradigm to create systems that interpret visual data and make intelligent decisions based on environmental interactions. The book focuses on ethical AI development and responsible programming, emphasizing the importance of developing AI that is fair, transparent, and accountable.

In this book you will learn how to:

- Explore Python basics and AI integration for real-world application and career advancement.
- Experience the power of Python in AI with practical machine learning techniques.
- Practice Python's deep learning tools for innovative AI solution development.
- Dive into NLP with Python to revolutionize data interpretation and communication strategies.
- Simple yet practical understanding of reinforcement learning for strategic AI decision-making.
- Uncover ethical AI development and frameworks, and concepts of responsible and trustworthy AI.
- Harness Python's capabilities for creating AI applications with a focus on fairness and bias.

Each chapter is designed to improve learning by including practical examples, case studies, and exercises that provide hands-on experience. This book is an excellent starting point for anyone interested in becoming an AI engineer, providing the necessary foundational knowledge and skills to delve into the fascinating world of artificial intelligence.

GitforGits

Prerequisites

Knowing simple python scripting and basics of data science is sufficient to enter the world of artificial intelligence. This book will aspire to make you an eligible professional to enter the world of AI Engineers and Data Scientist.

Codes Usage

Are you in need of some helpful code examples to assist you in your programming and documentation? Look no further! Our book offers a wealth of supplemental material, including code examples and exercises.

Not only is this book here to aid you in getting your job done, but you have our permission to use the example code in your programs and documentation. However, please note that if you are reproducing a significant portion of the code, we do require you to contact us for permission.

But don't worry, using several chunks of code from this book in your program or answering a question by citing our book and quoting example code does not require permission. But if you do choose to give credit, an attribution typically includes the title, author, publisher, and ISBN. For example, "Python AI Programming by Patrick J".

If you are unsure whether your intended use of the code examples falls under fair use or the permissions outlined above, please do not hesitate to reach out to us at support@gitforgits.com.

We are happy to assist and clarify any concerns.

Acknowledgement

I am grateful to GitforGits for their unwavering support and insightful advice throughout the entire process of writing this book. Their expertise and meticulous editing were critical in ensuring that this book is understandable and beneficial to readers at all levels of understanding. Furthermore, my heartfelt gratitude goes out to the entire publishing team, whose dedication has been instrumental in bringing this project to fruition, from meticulous copyediting to dynamic advertising. Their combined efforts have helped to shape the essence of this book.

Finally, I'd like to express my gratitude to everyone who has shown me unconditional love and encouragement throughout my life. Their support was crucial to the completion of this book. I appreciate your help with this endeavour and your continued interest in my career.

Chapter 1: Introduction to Artificial Intelligence

Historical Perspective of AI

Remember the old days when we didn't have smartphones constantly in our hands? That is a bit what it was like before AI. We had computers, but they were more like calculators on steroids. They could crunch numbers, follow instructions, but that is about it. No learning, no adapting – pretty basic, right? Think about those massive computers in the '60s and '70s – room-sized giants with less power than your smartphone. They did specific tasks, and to make them do something, you had to feed them a precise set of instructions. There was no "Hey Computer, learn this," it was all about programming every single detail.

Imagine writing a recipe for someone who doesn't know anything about cooking. You'd have to explain every step, right? That is how software was before AI. It couldn't think for itself. Programmers had to spell out everything. If there was a task you didn't foresee, well, the software wouldn't know what to do. We've had data for ages, way before AI. But back then, it was like having a goldmine and not knowing how to mine gold. We stored data in huge databases, mostly using it for record-keeping. It was like having a library of books but never reading them. We didn't have the tools to dig deeper and really understand what all that data could tell us.

We will discuss and understand about work life pre-AI. It was a lot more manual, even with computers. For example, think about a bank in the '80s. They had computers, but a lot of the work, like customer service or data analysis, was done by people, tediously sifting through information. There was a lot of potential for human error, and things took longer.

And then, there is the internet, or rather, the lack of it. The early internet was like a small town – everyone knew each other, and there wasn't much happening. We didn't have the vast ocean of online data and connectivity we have now. It's hard to imagine, right?

Lastly, think about AI back then. It was more a subject of sci-fi novels and movies than real life. People dreamt of intelligent machines, but it was just that – a dream. The technology, the data processing capabilities, they just weren't there yet.

It's wild to think about how different things were, isn't it? Just like looking back at how we lived without smartphones or streaming services. But, this background sets the perfect stage for the entry of AI – a game changer that took all these limitations and turned them on their head. It opened up a world of possibilities that we're still exploring today.

Transition to AI Era

So, we're looking at this fascinating shift from a world without AI to one where it's starting to take root. Imagine this period as the dawn of a new age. You know, like when people first saw airplanes and thought, "Wow, we can actually fly!" That is the kind of awe and wonder the early stages of AI brought along.

Before AI became a household name, technology and computing were progressing, but there was a missing piece – the ability for machines to learn and think, at least in a very basic sense. Computers were great at following orders, but they couldn't adapt or learn from their experiences. They were extremely efficient but very limited assistants. Then, slowly, things began to change. We started seeing computers not just as tools for specific tasks but as potential 'learners'. The idea was brewing that maybe, just maybe, we could teach computers to learn from data, to recognize patterns, and maybe even make decisions based on that learning. It was a big 'what if' that started turning the wheels of innovation.

This change didn't happen overnight. It was a gradual process, fueled by advancements in both hardware and software. On the hardware front, computers were becoming more powerful and affordable. They were no longer these room-sized behemoths but were getting smaller, faster, and more accessible. This meant more people could experiment, innovate, and push the boundaries of what was possible.

On the software side, we started developing more sophisticated algorithms. These weren't your standard, run-of-the-mill instructions but complex sets of rules that could take in data, process it, and learn from it. The early versions of these learning algorithms were pretty basic by today's standards, but back then, they were revolutionary. And, crucially, we had more data than ever before. The rise of the internet and digitization meant that data was being generated at an unprecedented scale. This was the fuel that AI needed – vast amounts of data to learn from.

So, picture this as the stage being set for AI's grand entrance. The tech was evolving, the algorithms were getting smarter, and the world was producing data in massive quantities. It was only a matter of time before all these elements came together, sparking the AI revolution we're part of today. It's quite a journey, isn't it? From basic computing to the cusp of AI – it sets the stage for some exciting developments. In our next section, we can explore how these elements converged to give birth to modern AI. What do you think about this transition period? It's like watching the pieces of a puzzle coming together, leading us to where we are now.

AI in Modern World

AI in Daily Life

Imagine waking up in the morning to your smart alarm, which analyzes your sleep patterns and wakes you up at the optimal time. You grab your phone, and there is your AI-powered news app, curating a news feed based on your interests. Even the mundane task of driving to work is transformed by AI with traffic predictions and route optimizations from your navigation app. And we will not forget about personal assistants like Siri or Alexa, which have become household names, helping us with everything from setting reminders to controlling smart home devices.

This is just the tip of the iceberg. Healthcare is seeing revolutionary changes with AI-driven diagnostics and personalized treatment plans. Retail experiences are more customized than ever, thanks to AI analyzing shopping habits. Even in education, AI provides personalized learning experiences, adapting to each student's unique learning curve.

AI in Business Operations

Consider switching gears to the business world. Companies of all sizes are harnessing AI for a competitive edge. One of the most significant impacts is on customer service. Chatbots and virtual assistants, powered by AI, are handling customer inquiries 24/7, providing instant, personalized responses. This not only improves customer experience but also reduces operational costs.

In marketing, AI is a game-changer. It's analyzing consumer behavior, market trends, and social media to tailor marketing strategies. This level of analysis was unthinkable a decade ago. AI is also revolutionizing supply chain management by predicting demand, optimizing inventory, and reducing delivery times.

Then there is the financial sector. AI-driven algorithms are used for everything from fraud detection to personalized financial advice. The precision and efficiency AI brings to these areas significantly enhance both security and customer experience.

AI for Decision Making

One of the most exciting aspects of AI is its role in decision-making. Gone are the days of solely relying on human intuition for business decisions. AI algorithms analyze vast amounts of data, uncovering insights and patterns that humans might overlook. This data-driven approach leads to more informed, strategic decisions.

The impact of AI in decision-making is particularly evident in sectors like manufacturing and healthcare, where precision and efficiency are paramount. In manufacturing, the application of AI for predictive maintenance is a game-changer. These sophisticated AI systems can predict potential machinery malfunctions before they happen. This foresight allows for timely maintenance, significantly reducing unexpected downtime and associated costs. It's a proactive approach, transforming maintenance from a reactive task to a strategic function that enhances productivity and longevity of equipment.

In healthcare, AI's role is nothing short of transformative. Healthcare professionals are now supported by AI systems that provide comprehensive analyses of patient data. These systems are designed to process vast amounts of patient information, from medical history to current symptoms, and suggest treatment plans. This is especially crucial in scenarios where time is of the essence, and the margin for error is minimal. AI assists in making critical life-saving decisions, offering recommendations that are data-driven and thus, potentially more accurate and effective.

AI in Innovation and Product Development

Product development has been transformed by AI. Companies are using AI to analyze market trends and consumer feedback, guiding them in developing products that meet precise market needs. AI even plays a role in the design process, with algorithms suggesting design modifications and improvements.

In software development, AI's role is increasingly pivotal. Quality assurance and testing, traditionally time-consuming phases in software development, are being revolutionized by AI. AI algorithms can swiftly identify potential issues, bugs, and areas for improvement in software, doing so with a precision and speed unattainable by manual testing. This capability significantly shortens the development cycle, enabling faster rollouts of more polished, user-friendly software products. It also allows human developers to focus on more complex, creative tasks, pushing the boundaries of what's possible in software development.

AI and Data Analytics

The heart of AI's impact lies in data analytics. With the exponential growth of data, AI is the key to unlocking its potential. Businesses use AI to analyze customer data, gaining insights into preferences and behaviors. This data is then used to personalize products and services, enhancing customer satisfaction.

In sports, AI offers coaches and athletes insights that are pivotal for optimizing training regimens and developing game strategies. By examining vast amounts of data on player performance, including physical fitness, skill levels, and in-game tactics, AI algorithms can identify areas for improvement and strengths to capitalize on. This personalized approach ensures that athletes are trained more effectively, leading to enhanced performance and better outcomes in competitions.

In agriculture, farmers are utilizing AI to make informed decisions about crop management, significantly improving agricultural productivity. AI systems can predict the most favorable planting times, considering factors like weather patterns, soil conditions, and historical crop performance. This precision farming approach helps in maximizing yield and reducing waste. Furthermore, AI is instrumental in monitoring soil health, using sensors and data analytics to provide real-time information on soil moisture, nutrient levels, and other critical factors. This information enables farmers to adjust their cultivation practices proactively, ensuring optimal growth conditions for their crops.

AI in Automation and Efficiency

AI's proficiency in handling routine and repetitive tasks has been a significant boon, marking a new era of efficiency and productivity. This automation frees human resources from mundane tasks, allowing them to focus on more creative, strategic, and complex activities. The value of AI in business automation is not confined to simple tasks; its impact is profound in automating intricate processes across various domains.

In fields like law and finance, AI is transforming operations by automating complex tasks such as document analysis and data processing. These sectors deal with vast amounts of data, where precision and speed are crucial. AI algorithms can sift through documents, extract relevant information, and analyze data with a level of speed and accuracy that is simply unattainable by humans. This capability not only accelerates the workflow but also minimizes errors, leading to more reliable and efficient outcomes. It allows professionals in these fields to focus on more nuanced aspects of their work, like strategy and client relations, while AI handles the data-intensive tasks.

The manufacturing sector is witnessing a similar revolution with the integration of AI. AI-powered robots are increasingly being employed in factories, working alongside human workers. This collaboration has enhanced efficiency and safety in manufacturing processes. AI robots can perform high-precision tasks, handle hazardous materials, and operate in environments that are unsafe for humans. This not only boosts productivity but also significantly reduces the risk of accidents and injuries. The human workers, in turn, can focus on supervisory roles, quality control, and other critical aspects that require human judgment and creativity.

AI in Healthcare

Healthcare deserves special mention. AI is revolutionizing this field in profound ways. From early diagnostics of diseases like cancer to robotic surgeries, AI is enhancing the quality and accessibility of healthcare. It's also personalizing patient care, with AI algorithms suggesting customized treatment plans based on individual patient data.

While the benefits of AI are immense, it's important to consider the ethical implications. Issues like data privacy, bias in AI algorithms, and the impact on employment are areas of active discussion and regulation. Ensuring that AI is used responsibly and ethically is crucial.

As we look to the future, the possibilities of AI are boundless. We're talking about AI collaborating with humans in creative fields like art and music, AI in environmental conservation, and even in space exploration. The convergence of AI with other emerging technologies like quantum computing and the Internet of Things (IoT) is set to create innovations we can't even imagine yet.

Key Concepts in Artificial Intelligence

Understanding Machine Learning

Machine Learning is the cornerstone of modern AI, fundamentally altering how we build software. In traditional programming, we code explicit rules. With ML, we feed data into algorithms, and they learn from this data. Think of it as teaching a child through examples. We show the child several pictures of cats and dogs, and over time, they learn to distinguish between the two. Similarly, we feed an ML algorithm lots of data (like pictures of cats and dogs), and it learns to recognize patterns in this data.

ML breaks down into three main types:

Supervised Learning

Supervised Learning is akin to a guided learning process. In this approach, the algorithm is trained on a labeled dataset. This dataset contains input-output pairs, where the desired output (label) is known. The algorithm's job is to learn a mapping between the inputs and outputs. Think of it like teaching a child with flashcards. Each card has a picture (input) and a name (output). Over time, the child learns to associate pictures with names. Similarly, a supervised learning algorithm learns to predict the output from new inputs.

Supervised learning excels in classification (categorizing data into classes) and regression (predicting continuous values) tasks. It's used in facial recognition systems (classifying faces), in predicting housing prices (regression), and even in medical diagnoses where symptoms are inputs and diseases are outputs.

Unsupervised Learning

Unsupervised Learning involves training the algorithm on data without any labels. The goal is to discover hidden patterns or structures within the data. It's like giving someone a mixed jigsaw puzzle and asking them to find patterns or groupings. The algorithm might identify clusters of similar data points (cluster analysis) or find the underlying structure (dimensionality reduction).

Unsupervised learning is crucial in market segmentation, where businesses identify different customer groups. It's also used in anomaly detection, like identifying fraudulent transactions in banking.

Reinforcement Learning

Reinforcement Learning is unique. An agent learns to make decisions by performing actions in an environment and receiving feedback in the form of rewards or penalties. It's similar to training a pet. When the pet performs a desirable action, it gets a treat (reward); otherwise, it might receive a mild reprimand (penalty). The pet learns to repeat actions that lead to treats.

Reinforcement Learning is at the heart of AI in gaming and robotics. It's used in training algorithms to play complex games like Go or Chess and for developing autonomous vehicles, where the vehicle learns to navigate and make driving decisions.

Each of the aforementioned types serves a distinct purpose. Supervised learning is highly effective for tasks involving classification and regression. Unsupervised learning is well-suited for uncovering latent patterns in data. Reinforcement learning is employed in situations where an autonomous entity, such as a robot or a self-driving car, needs to make decisions. The impact of Machine Learning is extensive and diverse. ML algorithms are utilized in healthcare to facilitate disease diagnosis and forecast patient outcomes. Within the realm of finance, these tools are employed for the purpose of detecting fraudulent activities and evaluating potential risks. Machine learning (ML) is utilized in marketing to gain insights into consumer behavior and tailor advertisements to individual preferences. Machine learning has a pervasive influence on various aspects of our lives, encompassing everything from the personalized recommendations we receive on streaming platforms to the management of online customer service chats.

Deep Learning

Deep Learning, a subset of Machine Learning, has taken AI to new heights. Inspired by the structure and function of the human brain, Deep Learning uses artificial neural networks. These networks, composed of layers of interconnected nodes (or 'neurons'), can learn and make intelligent decisions.

Neural Networks, particularly in Deep Learning, are inspired by the human brain's structure and function.

- Layers and Neurons: A typical neural network has an input layer, several hidden layers, and an output layer. Each layer consists of units (neurons) that perform computations. Data is fed into the input layer, processed through hidden layers (each layer extracting features and patterns), and the final output is generated.
- Learning Process: Neural networks learn by adjusting the weights of connections between neurons. This learning occurs during the training process, where the network iteratively adjusts these weights to minimize the difference between its predictions and the actual outcomes.

Deep Learning shines in handling vast amounts of unstructured data. For instance, consider image recognition. Traditional ML algorithms struggle here, but Deep Learning excels. By processing data through its multiple layers, a Deep Learning model can identify and understand complex patterns in images.

Applications of Deep Learning

Deep Learning's applications are groundbreaking. In autonomous vehicles, Deep Learning algorithms process and interpret the sensory input needed to navigate safely. In language processing, models like GPT (from OpenAI) use Deep Learning to understand and generate human-like text. Deep Learning is also pivotal in medical image analysis, helping to detect diseases like cancer more accurately and earlier than ever before.

Deep Learning has spurred numerous breakthroughs across various fields:

- Computer Vision: From facial recognition systems to medical imaging analysis, deep learning algorithms excel at interpreting and understanding visual data.
- Natural Language Processing (NLP): Tools like translation services, voice recognition systems, and chatbots leverage deep learning for understanding and generating human language.
- Autonomous Vehicles: Deep Learning is crucial in processing and interpreting the vast amounts of sensory data required for self-driving cars.
- Personalized Recommendations: Streaming services like Netflix use deep learning to analyze your viewing habits and recommend shows you might like.

The future of ML and Deep Learning holds immense promise. We are progressing towards the adoption of increasingly efficient and powerful models that necessitate a reduced amount of data and offer enhanced interpretability. This advancement will persist in transforming industries such as healthcare, automotive, finance, and beyond.

Python for AI

Python has emerged as the go-to language for AI and Machine Learning, and for good reasons. It strikes a perfect balance between simplicity and power, offering an easy-to-understand syntax with robust capabilities. Python acts like a bridge, making the complex world of AI accessible to developers. The real power of Python in AI lies in its vast ecosystem of libraries and frameworks. These tools abstract the complexities, allowing you to focus on solving AI problems rather than getting bogged down with technical details.

NumPy and Pandas for Data Handling

At its essence, NumPy provides a strong and reliable array structure. This structure is essential for executing intricate numerical computations, which are widespread in artificial intelligence tasks. NumPy arrays enable efficient and streamlined operations on large datasets, enabling vectorization and broadcasting to reduce code complexity. This simplification is of great value in the field of artificial intelligence, where the ability to efficiently handle multidimensional data and perform mathematical operations is crucial.

Pandas enhances the data manipulation and analysis capabilities by introducing the DataFrame structure, which complements NumPy. Pandas DataFrames are specifically designed to efficiently manage a wide range of data types, including numerical, categorical, and time-series data. Pandas' versatility renders it an essential tool in the data scientist's arsenal. It streamlines tasks such as data cleansing, manipulation, and consolidation, facilitating the preprocessing of data for AI modeling. Furthermore, Pandas' capacity to effortlessly import data from diverse sources and its intuitive management of missing data are essential for preserving data integrity, a pivotal factor in artificial intelligence.

Matplotlib and Seaborn for Data Visualization

Matplotlib is a fundamental tool in Python for creating a wide range of visualizations, including static, animated, and interactive ones. The main advantage of this tool is its capacity to provide precise manipulation over nearly every aspect of a plot or graph, encompassing plot type, color scheme, labels, and scales. Matplotlib's high degree of customization renders it an indispensable tool for AI practitioners, who frequently require the ability to communicate intricate data insights in a lucid and easily understandable manner. Matplotlib provides developers with the capability to customize their visual output according to their specific requirements, whether it involves line plots, scatter plots, bar charts, histograms, or any other type of visualization.

Seaborn enhances the existing capabilities of Matplotlib and introduces specialized features to meet the requirements of statistical data visualization. It excels in managing intricate datasets and generating visual representations that can unveil concealed structures and patterns within the data. Seaborn is particularly attractive to individuals who require a rapid and efficient means of exploring and comprehending their data, due to its focus on aesthetics and its capacity to produce more refined and informative plots with minimal code. The integration of Plotly with Pandas DataFrames streamlines the task of generating informative and visually appealing visualizations, rendering it highly popular among data scientists and AI experts.

Scikit-Learn for Machine Learning

Scikit-Learn is based on the foundational libraries of NumPy, SciPy, and matplotlib. It seamlessly incorporates these libraries to create a unified and robust environment for machine learning tasks. The library's design is user-friendly, allowing beginners to easily use it, while also being powerful enough to handle intricate machine learning tasks. It efficiently reduces the obstacle for entering the field of machine learning, making advanced data analysis tools accessible to a wider audience.

Scikit-Learn provides a wide variety of both supervised and unsupervised learning algorithms. Scikit-Learn includes a diverse range of tools, ranging from traditional algorithms such as linear regression, support vector machines, and decision trees, to more sophisticated techniques like clustering, dimensionality reduction, and ensemble methods. The ability to adapt and apply various machine learning techniques and models is a significant advantage of this system.

TensorFlow and PyTorch for Deep Learning

TensorFlow is notable for its extensive and adaptable ecosystem, encompassing a wide range of tools and libraries for diverse machine learning applications. The capacity to manage extensive and intricate machine learning tasks is unrivaled. TensorFlow's architecture is specifically engineered for distributed computing, allowing it to efficiently handle substantial datasets and execute demanding calculations across numerous CPUs and GPUs. This renders it a perfect selection for applications necessitating substantial computational capacity, such as the training of extensive neural networks and the management of extensive data pipelines. TensorFlow also provides TensorFlow Lite, which is designed for mobile and embedded devices, thus extending its capabilities to edge computing.

PyTorch provides a more intuitive and interactive approach to deep learning due to its dynamic computation graph. This functionality enables real-time modifications to the graph, which is especially advantageous for research and development endeavors that prioritize adaptability and efficiency. PyTorch's design is exceptionally user-friendly, facilitating the translation of developers' ideas into code. Additionally, its efficient memory utilization guarantees optimized resource management. PyTorch's characteristics have established it as a preferred choice for quickly creating initial versions and conducting experiments in the field of deep learning.

Keras for Neural Networks

An important advantage of Keras is its high level of user-friendliness. The API is designed in a way that is easy to understand for beginners and efficient for experienced users to perform complicated tasks. The user-friendly nature of this technology greatly reduces the obstacles for individuals to conduct experiments with neural networks, enabling a wider spectrum of people to engage in exploration and innovation within the field of artificial intelligence. Keras simplifies the process of constructing neural networks by abstracting away many of the intricate details, allowing users to concentrate on designing the architecture of their models.

Keras distinguishes itself with its modularity. The structure of this system consists of various fundamental components, such as layers, optimizers, and activation functions. These components can be flexibly combined to create and refine neural network models in a virtually unlimited number of ways. The modular approach allows for a more comprehensive comprehension of each element of a neural network and also offers the adaptability to customize models according to specific needs. Moreover, Keras's architecture promotes the process of experimentation, enabling developers to rapidly iterate and enhance their models.

Keras prioritizes extensibility to accommodate the requirement for customization in sophisticated deep learning endeavors. Users have the ability to effortlessly incorporate new modules as completely compatible components, thereby creating a dynamic and progressive tool. The extensibility of Keras guarantees its continued relevance and effectiveness in managing the dynamic and evolving fields of neural network design and deep learning research.

The remarkable feature of Keras is its capacity to expedite the creation of deep learning models for initial testing and development. It enables rapid development and testing of models, speeding up the rate of innovation in neural network research and application. Keras enables users to efficiently develop intricate neural networks by offering a user-friendly interface that sits atop robust deep learning backends.

Python isn't just about the tools; it's about the solutions it powers. Following are a few examples:

- Healthcare: Python is used to develop algorithms for predictive diagnostics, personalized medicine, and even robotic surgeries.
- Finance: From algorithmic trading to credit scoring and fraud detection, Python's AI capabilities are reshaping finance.
- Retail: Python helps in customer segmentation, inventory management, and personalized recommendation systems.
- Manufacturing: Python-driven AI optimizes production processes, predictive maintenance, and supply chain management.

As AI continues to evolve, Python's role in this domain is likely to grow even more significant. Its adaptability, coupled with a strong community, ensures that Python will remain at the forefront of AI innovations.

Setting up Python and AI Environment

Setting up Python in a Windows environment and then installing AI tools like TensorFlow and Keras is a straightforward process. It is easy to get both python and its AI tools installed and configured together.

Installing and Configuring Python on Windows

Download Python

- Visit the official Python website at python.org.
- Navigate to the Downloads section and choose the latest version for Windows. (I can see Python 3.12.1 in beta version is available to download.)
- Click on the below link to download the Windows installer: https://www.python.org/downloads/release/python-3121/

Install Python

- Once the installer is downloaded, run it.
- Very important: Make sure to check the box that says "Add Python 3.x to PATH" before you click "Install Now." This step ensures Python is added to your system environment variables, making it accessible from the command line.
- Follow the on-screen instructions to complete the installation.

Verify Installation

- Open Command Prompt.
- Type python --version and press Enter. You should see the Python version number that you installed, confirming that Python is correctly installed.

Installing TensorFlow and Keras

TensorFlow can be installed directly via pip, Python's package installer. Keras, as a high-level API, will be installed as part of TensorFlow.

Update pip

- In the Command Prompt, it's a good practice to update pip to the latest version. Type python -m pip install --upgrade pip and press Enter.

Install TensorFlow

- Type pip install tensorflow and press Enter. This command downloads TensorFlow and all its dependencies.
- TensorFlow installation can take some time as it's a large package.

Verify TensorFlow Installation

- Once the installation is complete, you can verify it by running a simple TensorFlow program.
- In the Command Prompt, type python to enter the Python interpreter.
- Then, type the following:

```
import tensorflow as tf
print(tf.__version__)
```

This should print the installed version of TensorFlow, confirming the installation.

Keras Check

- Since Keras is included with TensorFlow, you don't need a separate installation.
- To verify, in the Python interpreter, type:

```
import keras
```

- If there are no errors, Keras is successfully installed.
- Exit Python Interpreter:
- To exit the Python interpreter, type exit() and press Enter.

Coffee Preference Prediction App Overview

The coffee preference prediction app is designed to personalize the coffee experience for users. It aims to predict a user's coffee preferences based on various factors like taste preferences, consumption habits, and contextual data.

App Functionalities

- User Profiling: Users input their preferences, such as preferred coffee type, sweetness level, and caffeine strength.

- Contextual Factors: The app considers factors like time of day, weather, or user mood (if provided), as these can influence coffee choices.

- Preference Prediction: Using machine learning, the app predicts the user's coffee preference at a given moment, suggesting drinks they're likely to enjoy.

- Feedback Loop: Users rate or provide feedback on the suggestions, which the app uses to refine future predictions.

Dataset for Coffee Model

To train the machine learning model for this app, we need a dataset that captures the necessary information. We will outline what this dataset might look like:

Dataset Columns

- UserID: Unique identifier for each user.
- Age: Age of the user.
- Gender: Gender of the user.
- CoffeeType: Type of coffee (e.g., Espresso, Latte, Cappuccino, Americano).
- SweetnessLevel: Indicates the sweetness (e.g., None, Low, Medium, High).
- MilkType: Type of milk used (e.g., Whole, Skim, Soy, Almond).
- CaffeineStrength: Caffeine level (e.g., Decaf, Regular, Strong).
- TimeOfDay: When the coffee is consumed (e.g., Morning, Afternoon, Evening).
- DayOfWeek: Day of the week.
- Weather: Current weather condition (e.g., Sunny, Rainy, Cold, Hot).
- Mood: User's mood (optional, e.g., Happy, Stressed, Relaxed).
- PreviousOrder: The user's previous coffee order.
- UserRating: Rating given by the user to the coffee (1 to 5 stars).

Generating Dataset

For a real application, this data would be collected over time from user interactions. However, for our purposes, we can simulate a dataset. We can use Python to create a mock dataset that reflects these features. This simulated data will then be used to train and test our machine learning models.

You'll need libraries like Pandas, NumPy, and random for data manipulation and generation. These can be installed using pip, Python's package manager.

Creating Dataset with Python

Start by importing the necessary libraries:

```
import pandas as pd
import numpy as np
import random
```

Set a seed for reproducibility

```
np.random.seed(0)
```

Define the size of your sample, and then create data for each feature. For instance, you can generate data for user IDs, age, gender, coffee type preferences, etc., using random selections:

```
sample_size = 1000  # You can adjust this number

data = {
    'UserID': range(1, sample_size + 1),
    'Age': np.random.randint(18, 70, sample_size),
    'Gender': np.random.choice(['Male', 'Female', 'Other'], sample_size),
    'CoffeeType': np.random.choice(['Espresso', 'Latte', 'Cappuccino', 'Americano'],
sample_size),
    'SweetnessLevel': np.random.choice(['None', 'Low', 'Medium', 'High'], sample_size),
    'MilkType': np.random.choice(['Whole', 'Skim', 'Soy', 'Almond', 'None'], sample_size),
    # Add more columns as needed
```

```
}
```

Create a DataFrame

```
coffee_dataset = pd.DataFrame(data)
```

You can then view the dataset using coffee_dataset.head().

Using the Dataset

Once your dataset is ready, you can use it to train machine learning models. The dataset is now ready to explore different AI and ML techniques to predict coffee preferences based on the features in your dataset.

Understanding AI Project Lifecycle

Creating an AI application is an exciting journey that combines and revolves around several stages, each crucial to the development and success of the application.

Idea and Conceptualization

Understanding the Problem

The journey starts with identifying a problem or seizing an opportunity that can be effectively addressed with AI. This process involves a deep dive into the specific needs and challenges of the target audience. It's crucial to comprehend the nuances of the problem space, understanding not only the 'what' but also the 'why' of the situation. Grasping these aspects helps in pinpointing how AI can bring a transformative solution or improvement to the existing scenario.

Defining Objectives

Once the problem is understood, the next step is to define clear objectives for the AI application. This stage is about articulating what exactly the project aims to achieve. Objectives might range from enhancing efficiency and automating processes to providing personalized experiences or solving complex, unprecedented problems. These objectives need to be well-defined and strategic, ensuring they align with the overarching goals of the organization or the specific needs of the end-users.

Research and Feasibility Analysis

This phase involves thorough research into existing solutions and a comprehensive feasibility analysis. It's about understanding what has already been done in the domain, what worked, what didn't, and how the proposed AI solution can offer something different or better. A feasibility analysis is not just about the technical aspects, like data availability or algorithmic challenges, but also about practical considerations such as budget, resources, and timelines. This step is fundamental in ensuring that the AI project is grounded in reality, with a clear path towards successful implementation.

Data Collection and Preparation

Data Sources

The first step in this phase is identifying and gathering the right sources of data. These sources can vary widely depending on the nature of the AI project. They may include existing databases that house relevant historical data, data generated in real-time by users through various applications, sensor data capturing environmental or machine-based metrics, and online sources such as social media feeds or publicly available datasets. The key is to pinpoint sources that provide data which is not only relevant and rich in quality but also aligns with the ethical standards and privacy policies pertinent to the domain of the project.

Data Cleaning and Preprocessing

Once the data is collected, the next crucial step is cleaning and preprocessing it. Raw data is often far from perfect – it may contain errors, inconsistencies, or missing values that can skew the results of the AI model if not addressed. Cleaning the data involves processes such as identifying and rectifying errors, filling in missing values through various imputation methods, and removing duplicates that can lead to biased or redundant information in the dataset. After cleaning, preprocessing the data is essential to convert it into a format that is suitable for analysis and modeling. This step might include normalizing or scaling numerical data, encoding categorical data, and possibly transforming the data into a structured form that aligns with the requirements of the AI algorithms to be employed.

Choosing Right Tools and Technologies

Programming Language

The first step in this selection process is to choose a programming language that is well-suited for AI development. Python has become a particularly popular choice in the AI community due to its simplicity and readability, which makes it accessible to both beginners and experienced developers. Additionally, Python boasts a rich ecosystem of AI and machine learning libraries, which provides developers with a wealth of tools and functionalities to build, train, and deploy AI models effectively.

Frameworks and Libraries

The next step is to choose the right frameworks and libraries that align with the specific requirements of the AI project. For deep learning projects, TensorFlow, Keras, and PyTorch are among the most widely used frameworks. TensorFlow is known for its powerful and flexible capabilities for large-scale machine learning, Keras for its user-friendliness and modularity, particularly in designing neural networks, and PyTorch for its dynamic computation graph which allows for more flexibility in model building and iteration. The choice among these depends on various factors like the complexity of the project, the level of customization required, and the specific nature of the tasks the AI is expected to perform.

Development Environment

Setting up an effective development environment is the final step in this process. This involves installing the chosen programming language, frameworks, and libraries, and ensuring that they are all compatible and functioning seamlessly together. The development environment should also include tools for version control, such as Git, and, if required, integrated development environments (IDEs) like PyCharm or Jupyter Notebooks for Python. Additionally, depending on the project's scale, it may also be necessary to set up a more sophisticated environment with support for parallel computing and GPU acceleration, especially for tasks involving large datasets or complex neural networks.

Designing the AI Model

Selecting the AI Technique

The choice of AI technique is dictated by the nature of the problem at hand. If the problem involves pattern recognition or predictive analytics, machine learning might be the appropriate choice. For more complex tasks like image or speech recognition, deep learning could be more suitable. In cases involving language processing, natural language processing (NLP) is often the best fit. The key is to align the technique with the specific requirements and complexities of the problem.

Building the Model

The architecture of an AI model is its backbone. It involves deciding on the type of neural network most suitable for the task – be it a simple feedforward network for basic tasks, a convolutional neural network (CNN) for image processing, or a recurrent neural network (RNN) for time-series analysis. The configuration of layers and nodes within these networks, and how they are interconnected, forms the crux of the model's ability to learn and make predictions. This stage requires a careful balance between complexity and efficiency to ensure the model is capable but not overly resource-intensive.

Feature Engineering

Feature engineering is a critical process in model design, involving the identification and selection of the most relevant input variables (features) that the model will use. The quality and relevance of these features directly impact the model's performance. This process includes not only selecting the right features but also transforming and scaling them in a way that makes them most useful for the model. Effective feature engineering can significantly enhance a model's learning ability and accuracy in predictions or decision-making.

Training the AI Model

Feeding the Data

The prepared data, which has been meticulously collected, cleaned, and preprocessed, is now fed into the AI model. This data is the foundation upon which the model will learn and develop its capabilities. An essential practice in AI model training is dividing the data into distinct sets – typically, a training set and a testing set. The training set is used to train the model, while the testing set serves to evaluate its performance. This separation is crucial for assessing how well the model can generalize to new, unseen data.

Training Process

The heart of the training process is where the AI model is exposed to the training data, allowing it to learn and recognize patterns, correlations, and connections within the data. This learning is facilitated through various algorithms and techniques specific to the type of AI model being developed. During training, the model iteratively adjusts its parameters (like weights in neural networks) to minimize errors in its predictions or outputs. This process is often supervised by optimization algorithms that seek to reduce the difference between the model's predictions and the actual data outcomes.

Model Evaluation

After training, the model is evaluated using the testing set. This evaluation is crucial to understand how well the model performs when faced with data it hasn't seen during the training phase. Various metrics are employed to evaluate the model's performance. Accuracy measures the proportion of correct predictions, precision looks at the proportion of positive identifications that were actually correct, recall assesses the proportion of actual positives that were identified correctly, and the F1 score provides a balance between precision and recall. These metrics offer insights into different aspects of the model's performance, allowing developers to understand its strengths and areas for improvement.

Model Optimization and Tuning

Hyperparameter Tuning

Hyperparameter tuning is one of the most important aspects of model optimization. Hyperparameters are the configuration settings used to structure the AI model, and they play a significant role in determining the model's performance. Unlike model parameters, which are learned during training, hyperparameters are set prior to the training process and require careful adjustment to optimize the model. This process can involve tuning various aspects such as the learning rate, which determines the step size at each iteration while moving toward a minimum of a loss function, or the architecture of the model itself, like the number of layers and the number of units in each layer in a neural network. The goal is to find the optimal combination of hyperparameters that results in the best performance of the model on a given task.

Cross-validation

Cross-validation is a technique used to evaluate the effectiveness of the model and to ensure that it is not overly dependent on the particular split of the training and testing data. In cross-validation, the data set is divided into multiple smaller sets, and the model is trained and evaluated multiple times, each time using a different set as the testing set and the remaining data as the training set. This approach provides a more comprehensive understanding of the model's performance and helps in identifying issues such as overfitting or underfitting.

Handling Overfitting or Underfitting

Overfitting occurs when a model performs well on the training data but fails to generalize to new, unseen data. Underfitting, on the other hand, happens when a model is too simple to capture the complexity of the data and therefore performs poorly even on the training data. To address overfitting, techniques such as adding dropout layers in neural networks, increasing the amount of training data, or using regularization methods can be employed. For underfitting, making the model more complex by adding more layers or units, or choosing a more powerful model can be effective strategies.

Integration and Deployment

Integration with Existing Systems

Integrating the AI model into the existing IT infrastructure or specific applications is a delicate process that requires careful planning and execution. This step involves ensuring that the AI model can communicate and function seamlessly with other parts of the system. It requires attention to compatibility with existing data formats, software components, and workflows. The integration must be done in a way that the AI model's inputs and outputs are properly aligned with the existing system's requirements. It may involve API development, creating middleware for communication, or modifying certain aspects of the existing systems to accommodate the AI model.

Deployment

Deployment is the process of placing the AI model into a production environment where it can start performing its intended tasks. This could mean deploying the model on cloud platforms, which offer scalability and flexibility, in-house servers, which might provide more control over the data and resources, or directly integrating it into an application. Deployment must consider aspects like load balancing, scalability, security, and data privacy. It's important to choose the right deployment strategy that aligns with the project's requirements and constraints.

Monitoring and Maintenance

Once deployed, continuous monitoring of the AI application is crucial. This involves tracking the application's performance, identifying any issues or bugs, and ensuring that it is functioning as expected. Monitoring can provide insights into how the AI model performs in real-world scenarios and can help identify areas for improvement. Alongside monitoring, regular maintenance is essential. This includes updating the model with new data, tweaking it to adapt to changes in the operational environment or user behavior, and fixing any issues that arise. Maintenance ensures that the AI application remains effective and efficient over time.

Testing and Quality Assurance

Functionality Testing

The primary objective of functionality testing is to verify that each feature of the AI application operates according to the specified requirements. This involves systematic testing of all functions, including user commands, data manipulation, searches, and operational workflows. During this phase, test cases are created to cover all possible scenarios, including edge cases, to ensure that the application behaves as expected in every situation. It's essential to identify and rectify any functional errors, glitches, or unexpected behavior in the application. Functionality testing is not limited to the AI model alone but extends to the entire application, including the user interface, integrations with other systems, and data processing pipelines.

Performance Testing

Performance testing assesses the application's speed, scalability, and reliability under various conditions. This includes testing the application's response time, speed of processing data, and its ability to handle large volumes of data or simultaneous requests. Scalability testing ensures that the application can accommodate growth, such as an increase in user numbers or data volume, without degradation in performance. Reliability testing involves ensuring the application is stable and consistently produces accurate and expected results over time.

User Testing

User testing is a key component of quality assurance, focusing on the end-users' interaction with the application. It provides insights into the application's usability, design, and overall user experience. This phase typically involves a group of end-users who use the application in real-world scenarios. Their feedback is crucial in identifying issues related to usability, understanding, and satisfaction. User testing helps in understanding how intuitive and efficient the application is from the user's perspective, allowing developers to make necessary adjustments to improve the overall user experience.

Ethical Considerations and Compliance

Data Privacy and Security

AI applications must adhere to relevant data privacy laws, such as the General Data Protection Regulation (GDPR) in the European Union or other local data protection regulations. This involves ensuring that the data collected and used by the AI is done so in a lawful, fair, and transparent manner. Protecting user data from unauthorized access, breaches, and other security threats is also equally paramount. This includes encrypting data, securing data transfers, and regularly updating security protocols. It's also important to have robust policies for data storage, processing, and sharing, ensuring that all practices comply with privacy laws and ethical standards.

Bias and Fairness

AI models can inadvertently learn and amplify biases present in their training data, leading to unfair or discriminatory outcomes. Regular checks for biases in the AI model are essential to identify and address any issues of fairness. To ensure ethical decision-making, steps must be taken to mitigate any identified biases. This might include diversifying the training data, adjusting the AI algorithms, or implementing fairness-aware modeling techniques. The goal is to create AI applications that are inclusive and equitable, providing fair and unbiased outcomes for all users.

This comprehensive overview of the stages involved in creating an AI application highlights the multifaceted nature of AI development. From the initial conceptualization to the final deployment and monitoring, each stage plays a critical role in shaping a successful, effective, and ethically responsible AI application.

Summary

In this chapter, we embarked on a comprehensive journey through the lifecycle of creating an AI application, a process that intertwines technical skill with creative vision. Beginning with the conceptualization phase, we underscored the importance of clearly defining the problem an AI solution is intended to solve. This initial stage is crucial as it sets the foundation and direction for the entire project. We delved into the significance of understanding user needs and conducting thorough research to ensure the feasibility and potential impact of the AI application. The idea is to bridge the gap between technological possibilities and practical needs, creating a solution that is not just innovative but also genuinely useful and user-centric.

Data collection and preparation then took center stage, highlighting its role as the cornerstone of any AI project. Quality and relevance of data directly influence the effectiveness of the AI model. We learned the intricacies of data sourcing, cleaning, and preprocessing, stressing the point that well-prepared data leads to more accurate and reliable AI models. This stage is often labor-intensive but is vital for laying a strong foundation for the AI system.

The selection of tools and technologies is another critical phase. We explored how Python has emerged as a preferred choice for AI development, thanks to its simplicity and the rich ecosystem of libraries and frameworks like TensorFlow and Keras. The process of designing, training, and optimizing the AI model was detailed, emphasizing the importance of choosing the right algorithms, adjusting hyperparameters, and employing techniques like cross-validation to enhance model performance. This is where the theoretical aspects of AI merge with practical implementation, and the true magic of AI begins to unfold.

Finally, the integration, deployment, and continuous maintenance of the AI application were learned. The importance of user interface design, rigorous testing, and quality assurance were highlighted, ensuring that the final product is not only technically sound but also user-friendly and reliable. Post-deployment, the application requires ongoing monitoring and updating to remain effective, catering to changing user needs and adapting to new data. Ethical considerations, particularly in terms of data privacy, security, and bias, were also brought to the forefront, reminding us that AI development is as much about technological innovation as it is about responsibility and ethical considerations.

CHAPTER 2: PYTHON FOR AI

Python Basics

Today, we will begin our exploration of Python by embarking on a journey through its fundamental aspects, beginning with the data structures. Python is a language that is widely used for a wide variety of applications, particularly in the rapidly developing field of artificial intelligence. Its success can be attributed to the fact that it is both straightforward and adaptable. It is essential for anyone who is interested in enhancing their programming skills or gaining a deeper understanding of artificial intelligence to have a fundamental understanding of Python.

Python Data Structures

At the heart of Python programming are data structures, integral components that store and handle data. This efficient management of data paves the way for effective access and modification, which is crucial in programming.

Lists

Picture lists as adaptable containers. They store various items, irrespective of their types, and keep them in order. For instance, creating a list of customer names is as simple as writing customers = ['Alice', 'Bob', 'Charlie']. What's special about lists is their mutability; they allow the addition, removal, or alteration of their elements.

Example:

```
# Creating a list
coffee_types = ['Espresso', 'Latte', 'Cappuccino']

# Accessing list elements
print(coffee_types[0])  # Output: Espresso

# Adding an element
coffee_types.append('Americano')
print(coffee_types)  # Output: ['Espresso', 'Latte', 'Cappuccino', 'Americano']
```

Tuples

Tuples are relatives of lists but with a twist: they are immutable. Once you create a tuple, like dimensions = (100, 50), it remains unchanged. This immutability makes them quicker and more reliable for read-only operations.

Dictionaries

Think of dictionaries as personal organizers. They pair data in a key-value format, much like a phone book. For example, a user's information might be stored as user = {'name': 'Alice', 'age': 30}, allowing for swift retrieval of data using unique keys.

Example:

```
# Creating a dictionary

user_profile = {'name': 'Alice', 'age': 29, 'favorite_coffee': 'Latte'}


# Accessing dictionary elements

print(user_profile['name'])  # Output: Alice


# Adding a new key-value pair

user_profile['loyalty_points'] = 120
```

Sets

Sets are collections of distinct elements. They shine in tasks like identifying unique items and performing set arithmetic. An example would be unique_users = {'Alice', 'Bob', 'Alice'}, which Python automatically translates to {'Alice', 'Bob'}.

Functions for Modularity

The reuse of code and modularization are both significantly aided by Python's functions. They are able to be invoked whenever it is necessary and encapsulate particular tasks.

Defining Functions

Using the def keyword, you can define a function. For instance, def greet(name): initiates a function that takes a name and performs a designated action.

Calling Functions

You call a function by its name and provide the necessary arguments, like greet('Alice').

Return Values

Functions can send back data using the return statement, enabling the use of this output elsewhere in your code.

Example:

```
# Defining a function
def greet(name):
    return f"Hello, {namc}!"

# Using the function
print(greet('Bob'))  # Output: Hello, Bob!
```

Loops

Loops in Python automate repetitive tasks, making them a cornerstone of efficient programming.

For Loops

These are ideal for going through sequences like lists or strings. The syntax for item in sequence: lets you access each element in turn.

Example:

```
# Iterating over a list
for coffee in coffee_types:
    print(f"I like {coffee}")
```

While Loops

These continue as long as a condition remains true. They are particularly useful when the number of iterations is unknown beforehand.

Example:

```
# Using a while loop
counter = 0
while counter < 3:
    print(f"Counter is {counter}")
    counter += 1
```

Loop Controls
break and continue dictate the flow of loops. break exits the loop, whereas continue skips to the next cycle.

Conditional Statements

Python utilizes conditional statements for executing code based on specific conditions.

Basic If-Else
In Python, the statement 'if condition:' followed by an indented block allows for the execution of code exclusively when the condition is true. For situations that do not meet the initial condition, the 'else:' clause is used to define an alternate set of instructions.

Example:

```
# If-else example
if user_profile['age'] > 30:
   print("30+ club")
else:
   print("Under 30 club")
```

Elif
This is shorthand for 'else if', allowing for sequential checking of multiple conditions.

Error Handling

Python employs try-except blocks for graceful error handling.

Try Block
This block acts as a safety net, allowing the program to test the potentially problematic code. If there is an error in the code enclosed within the try block, instead of halting the entire program, it gracefully transitions to a predefined error-handling routine.

Except Block
When an error occurs in the code within the try block, control is passed to the except block. This block contains code that is specifically designed to respond to and handle the error that was raised in the try block. The except block provides a way to gracefully manage errors, offering an alternative pathway for the program to execute when something goes wrong, instead of crashing

or producing incorrect results.

Example:

```
# Error handling example
try:
    print(user_profile['occupation'])
except KeyError:
    print("Occupation not found.")
```

File Handling

Python simplifies file operations, which are vital in AI and data-driven projects.

Opening Files

Use open(filename, mode) to start working with a file. Modes include 'r' for reading, 'w' for writing, etc.

Reading and Writing

Manipulate file contents with methods like .read() and .write().

Example:

```
# Writing to a file
with open('test.txt', 'w') as file:
    file.write("Hello, Python!")

# Reading from a file
with open('test.txt', 'r') as file:
    content = file.read()
    print(content)
```

Closing Files

Always close a file with file.close() or use a with statement for automatic closure.

With this foundation in Python basics, you're well-prepared for tackling data processing and manipulation tasks that are prevalent in AI projects. In the following sections, we will build upon these basics, venturing into how Python specifically caters to AI needs with its powerful libraries and frameworks. You'll see how these fundamentals form the building blocks

Data Analysis Overview

When exploring data analysis in Python, we come across two highly influential libraries: Pandas and NumPy. These libraries are essential for managing and analyzing data in Python, especially in the domains of AI and machine learning. While they were briefly covered in the previous section, this section will go into more detail about them.

Pandas at a Glance

Pandas is an open-source library providing high-performance, easy-to-use data structures, and data analysis tools. It's particularly well-suited for handling and analyzing structured data (like tables).

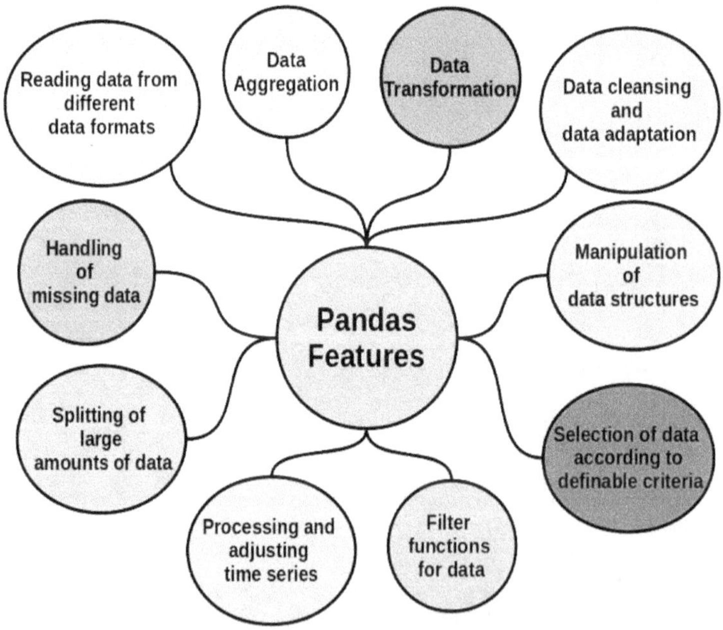

Fig 2.1 Features of Pandas

(Source: https://starship-knowledge.com/numpy-vs-pandas)

Core Features

- DataFrame: The primary data structure in Pandas. It's a two-dimensional, size-mutable, and potentially heterogeneous tabular data structure with labeled axes (rows and columns).

- Series: A one-dimensional labeled array capable of holding any data type.
- Handling Missing Data: Pandas is equipped to handle missing or NA values in data.
- Data Operations: Facilitates tasks like merging, reshaping, selecting, as well as data cleaning and preparation.
- Time Series: Pandas has extensive capabilities and features for working with time series data.

Data Analysis with Pandas

Reading Data

Pandas supports various file formats like CSV, Excel, SQL, and JSON. For example, pd.read_csv('file.csv') reads a CSV file into a DataFrame.

Data Exploration

Functions like head(), describe(), and info() provide a quick overview of the data.

Data Cleaning

Includes handling missing values, dropping or filling NA values, and data type conversions.

Data Manipulation

This includes filtering, sorting, grouping, and aggregating data. For instance, finding the average sale per coffee type.

Consider you have a dataset of coffee shop sales. Pandas allows you to easily read this data from a file, manipulate it, perform aggregations (like total sales per product), and prepare it for further analysis or visualization.

Introduction to NumPy

NumPy, short for Numerical Python, is a fundamental package for scientific computing in Python. It provides a high-performance multidimensional array object and tools for working with these arrays.

Core Features

- Multidimensional Arrays: NumPy arrays (ndarray), which are faster and more compact than Python lists.
- Mathematical Functions: NumPy provides many mathematical operations to perform computations on arrays.
- Broadcasting: A powerful mechanism that allows NumPy to work with arrays of different shapes during arithmetic operations.

- Linear Algebra: In-built support for various linear algebra operations, which is crucial in many AI algorithms.

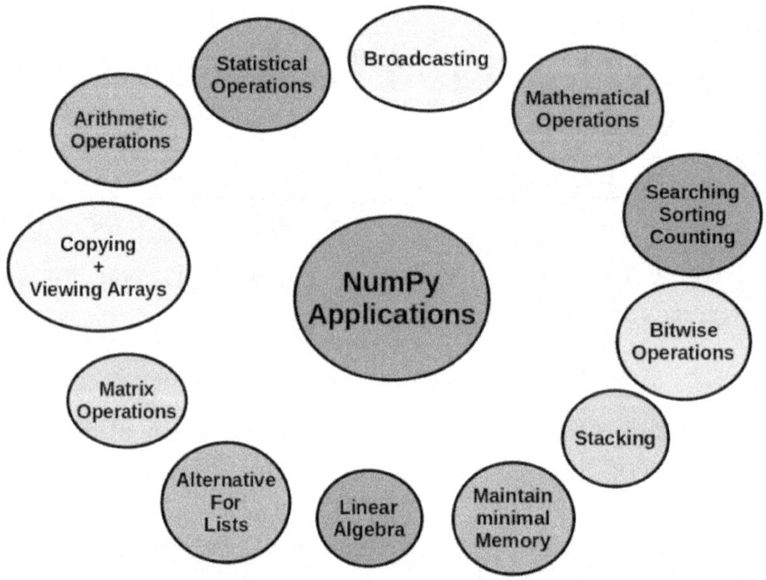

Fig 2.2 Numpy Applications

(Source: https://starship-knowledge.com/numpy-vs-pandas)

In AI, particularly in neural networks, you often deal with high-dimensional data. NumPy provides an efficient way to store and manipulate this data. For instance, image data can be represented as multidimensional arrays and processed using NumPy.

Numerical Computations with NumPy

Array Operations

Perform operations like addition, subtraction, and multiplication on arrays.

Statistical Analysis

NumPy offers functions like mean(), median(), std() for statistical analysis of data.

Linear Algebra

Operations like matrix multiplication, finding eigenvalues, and solving linear equations.

Pandas and NumPy both are often used in tandem. For instance, in a machine learning project, you might use Pandas for data exploration and manipulation, and then convert the Pandas

DataFrame into a NumPy array to feed into a machine learning model.

Consider our coffee app as a practical example of predicting customer preferences. To begin, you'd use Pandas to read historical customer data and clean and preprocess it (such as handling missing values, encoding categorical variables, and so on). Then, you can use NumPy to perform any necessary numerical computations or to reshape the data into a format suitable for machine learning models.

Sample Program: Using Numpy and Pandas

We will create a sample program that demonstrates the power of Pandas and NumPy in data analysis. For this, we will create a hypothetical dataset that could represent customer orders in a coffee shop. The dataset includes columns like OrderID, Product, Quantity, Price, and Date.

Creating a Sample Dataset

For the sake of demonstration, we will import the libraries and create a sample DataFrame directly in Python.

```
# Import libraries
import pandas as pd
import numpy as np


# Sample data
data = {
    'OrderID': [1, 2, 3, 4, 5],
    'Product': ['Espresso', 'Latte', 'Cappuccino', 'Americano', 'Latte'],
    'Quantity': [1, 2, 1, 3, 2],
    'Price': [3.50, 4.50, 4.00, 3.00, 4.50],
    'Date': pd.to_datetime(['2021-01-01', '2021-01-01', '2021-01-02', '2021-01-02', '2021-
01-03'])
}


# Creating a DataFrame
df = pd.DataFrame(data)
```

Basic Data Exploration

```
# Display the first few rows of the DataFrame
print(df.head())

# Basic statistics of the dataset
print(df.describe())

# Information about data types and null values
print(df.info())
```

Data Manipulation with Pandas

```
# Adding a new column for total price
df['TotalPrice'] = df['Quantity'] * df['Price']

# Filtering rows: Selecting only 'Latte' orders
latte_orders = df[df['Product'] == 'Latte']

# Grouping data and aggregating
daily_sales = df.groupby(df['Date']).sum()
```

Data Analysis with NumPy and Pandas

```
# Calculate the average quantity sold
average_quantity = np.mean(df['Quantity'])

# Find the day with the highest sales
max_sales_day = daily_sales['TotalPrice'].idxmax()
```

```
# Correlation between Quantity and Price
correlation = df['Quantity'].corr(df['Price'])
```

Basic Visualization

If you have matplotlib installed (pip install matplotlib), you can add basic visualizations. If not, we will anyways learn to use it along with seaborn in the next section.

```
import matplotlib.pyplot as plt


# Plotting daily sales
daily_sales['TotalPrice'].plot(kind='bar')
plt.title('Daily Sales')
plt.xlabel('Date')
plt.ylabel('Total Sales')
plt.show()
```

This sample program is a primer into the world of data analysis with Pandas and NumPy. The power of these libraries lies in their ability to handle, manipulate, and analyze data efficiently.

Data Visualization Overview

Visualizing data is an integral part of the AI process – from initial data exploration to model evaluation and interpretation of results. Both, Matplotlib and Seaborn, offers powerful tools for visualizing data, allowing you to convey complex concepts and relationships in a way that is accessible to both technical and non-technical audiences. While they were briefly covered in the previous section, this section will go into more detail about them.

Introduction to Matplotlib

Matplotlib is a comprehensive library for creating static, animated, and interactive visualizations in Python. It's highly customizable and capable of producing a wide variety of plots and charts.

Core Features

- Plot Variety: Matplotlib can create line plots, scatter plots, bar charts, histograms, pie charts, and many more.
- Customization: Almost every element of a plot can be customized – from colors and styles

to axes and labels.

- Multi-Plot Interface: You can create figures with multiple subplots, each with its own plot.

A typical use of Matplotlib in data analysis could involve creating a line plot to show trends over time or a histogram to display the distribution of a dataset.

Introduction to Seaborn

Seaborn is built on top of Matplotlib and provides a high-level interface for drawing attractive and informative statistical graphics. It's particularly suited for exploring and understanding complex datasets.

Core Features

- Advanced Plots: Seaborn makes it easy to create complex plots like heatmaps, pair plots, and violin plots.
- Statistical Plotting: Many of Seaborn's plotting functions integrate statistical model fitting, such as regression lines.
- Theming: Seaborn comes with built-in themes for styling Matplotlib graphics, making it simpler to create visually appealing plots.

In AI, you might use Seaborn for visualizing the distribution of data or the relationship between different variables, which is crucial in feature selection and model evaluation.

We will look at how Matplotlib and Seaborn facilitate our understanding of AI.

Setting Up Matplotlib and Seaborn

If Matplotlib and Seaborn aren't already installed in your Python environment, they can be easily added using pip:

```
pip install matplotlib seaborn
```

We shall assume we have a dataset representing sales data for a coffee shop, including the types of coffee sold, quantities, and sales figures over a week.

Import Libraries

```
import matplotlib.pyplot as plt
import seaborn as sns
```

```
import pandas as pd
```

Creating a Sample DataFrame

For demonstration, we will create a DataFrame directly in Python.

```
# Sample data
data = {
    'Day': ['Mon', 'Tue', 'Wed', 'Thu', 'Fri', 'Sat', 'Sun'],
    'Espresso': [75, 50, 60, 80, 90, 120, 110],
    'Latte': [200, 180, 190, 210, 230, 300, 280],
    'Cappuccino': [150, 130, 140, 170, 180, 250, 220]
}

# Creating a DataFrame
df = pd.DataFrame(data)
```

Basic Line Plot using Matplotlib

We shall create a line plot to visualize the sales of different coffee types throughout the week.

```
plt.figure(figsize=(10, 6))
plt.plot(df['Day'], df['Espresso'], label='Espresso', marker='o')
plt.plot(df['Day'], df['Latte'], label='Latte', marker='o')
plt.plot(df['Day'], df['Cappuccino'], label='Cappuccino', marker='o')
plt.title('Coffee Sales Throughout the Week')
plt.xlabel('Day of the Week')
plt.ylabel('Number of Cups Sold')
plt.legend()
plt.show()
```

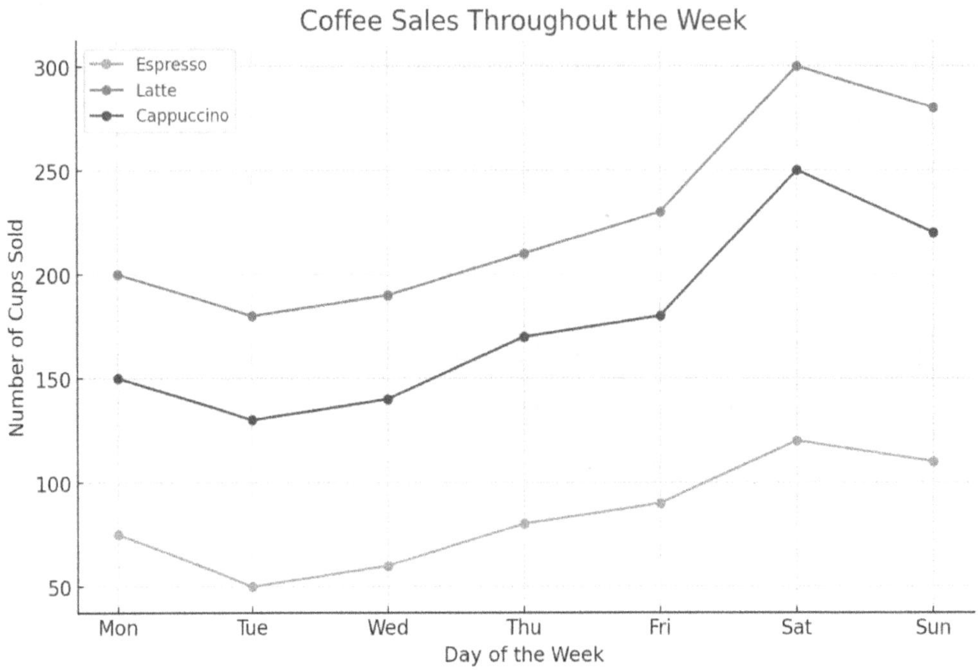

Fig 2.3 Line Plot

The above line plot shows the trends in coffee sales across the week. It's clear which days are busiest and which coffee type is most popular. This plot shows the trends in sales for Espresso, Latte, and Cappuccino across the week. The use of different colors and markers helps distinguish between the coffee types. It's a straightforward way to observe sales patterns and identify which days are the busiest or which coffee type is most popular.

Creating a Heatmap using Seaborn

Heatmaps are excellent for visualizing patterns in data matrices. We shall visualize the correlation between different coffee types.

```
# Calculating correlations
corr = df.drop('Day', axis=1).corr()

# Creating a heatmap
plt.figure(figsize=(8, 6))
sns.heatmap(corr, annot=True, cmap='coolwarm')
plt.title('Correlation between Coffee Types')
```

```
plt.show()
```

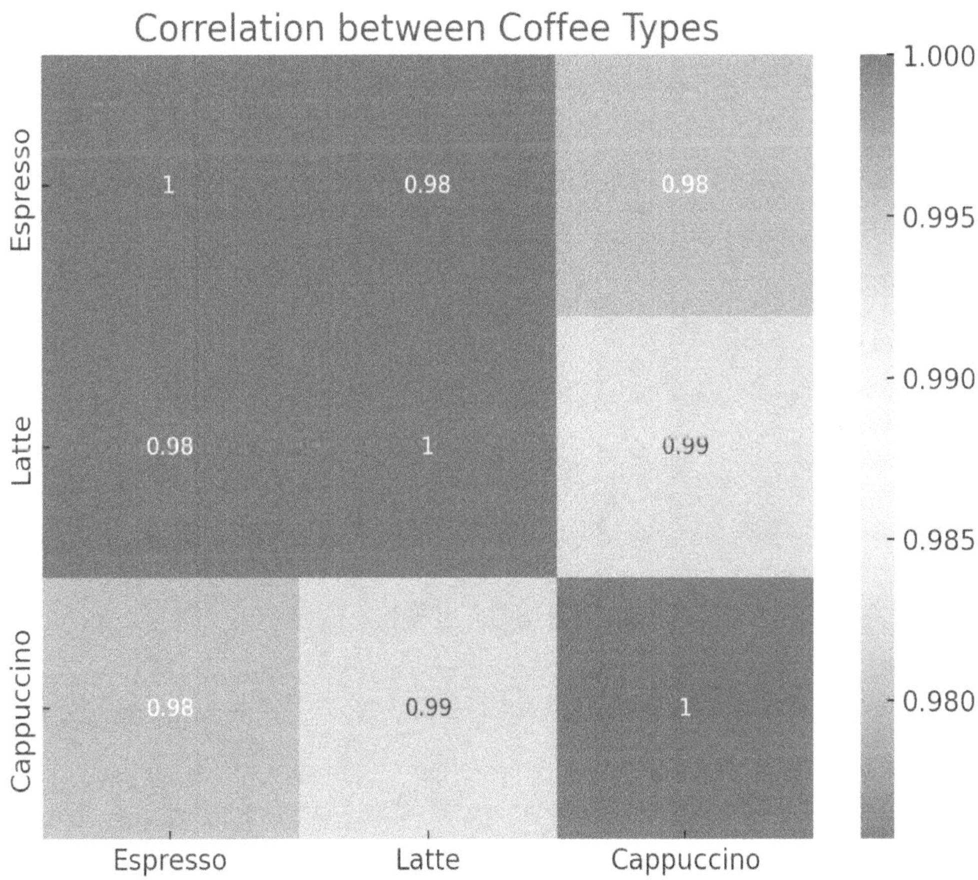

Fig 2.4 Heatmap

The above heatmap illustrates how sales of different coffee types correlate with each other. A high positive correlation indicates that when sales of one type increase, sales of another type also tend to increase. The heatmap visualizes the correlation matrix of the coffee types. This is particularly useful to understand how sales of one type of coffee may relate to others. For instance, a high positive value indicates a strong positive correlation, suggesting that customers who buy one type of coffee might also be inclined to buy another.

Bar Plot using Seaborn

Bar plots are useful for comparing quantities. We shall compare the total weekly sales of each coffee type.

```
# Preparing data for bar plot
total_sales = df.drop('Day', axis=1).sum()

# Creating a bar plot
plt.figure(figsize=(8, 6))
sns.barplot(x=total_sales.index, y=total_sales.values)
plt.title('Total Weekly Sales of Coffee Types')
plt.xlabel('Coffee Type')
plt.ylabel('Total Cups Sold')
plt.show()
```

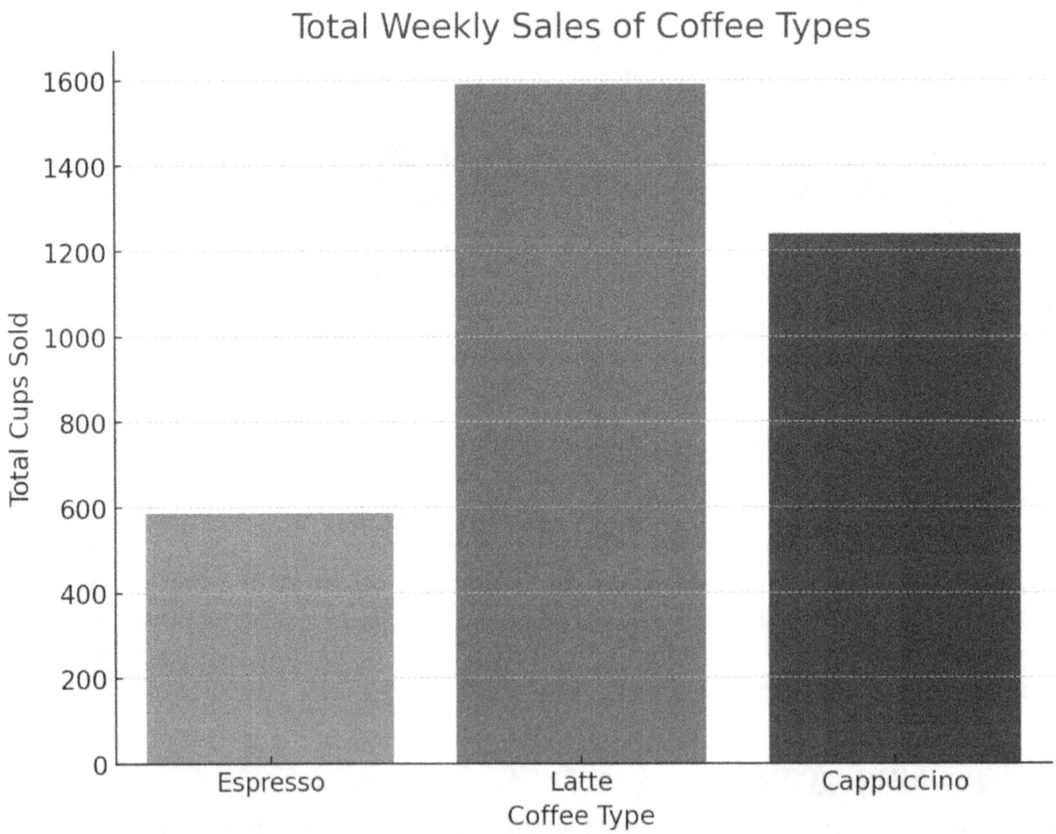

Fig 2.5 Bar Plot

The above bar plot provides a clear comparison of the total sales of each coffee type over the week. It's an effective visualization for comparing quantities and quickly identifying which coffee type is the best seller.

Pair Plot using Seaborn

A pair plot allows us to see both distribution of single variables and relationships between two variables. We shall use it to visualize our coffee data.

```
sns.pairplot(df.drop('Day', axis=1))
plt.show()
```

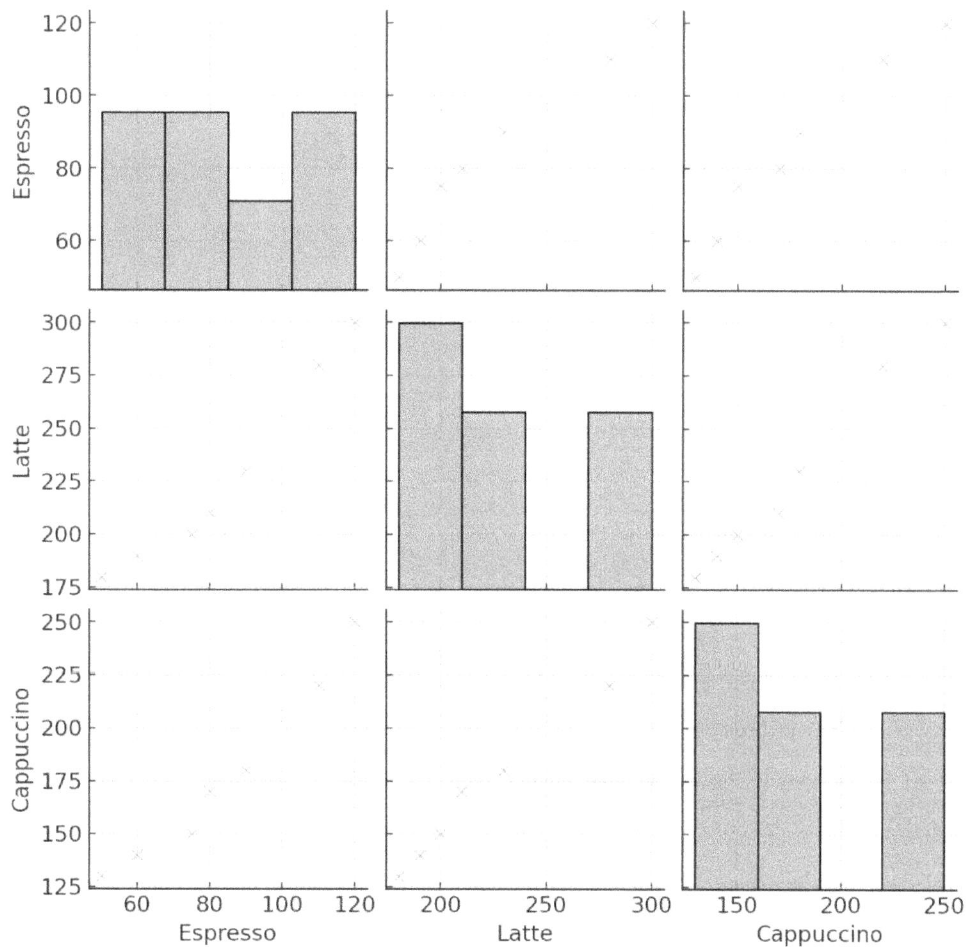

Fig 2.6 Pair Plot

The above pair plot offers a comprehensive view of the dataset, showcasing the distribution of each type of coffee and the relationships between them. Each subplot shows the relationship between two types of coffee, along with histograms showing the distribution of sales for each type. This visualization is particularly useful for identifying patterns and relationships in multi-dimensional data.

Through various types of plots and visualizations, both libraries enable us to uncover patterns, trends, and correlations in data, which are crucial for making informed decisions in AI and machine learning projects.

Error Handling in Python

Error handling is an important aspect of programming, especially in AI applications where data and environments can be unpredictable and variable. Python provides robust error handling mechanisms, primarily through the use of try-except blocks, which aid in dealing with unexpected situations gracefully without crashing the program. We will look at some of the most common AI development scenarios and how to handle basic errors in each one.

Common Errors

Data File Handling

When reading data files, there is a risk the file might not exist, be corrupt, or be in an unexpected format.

Solution: Use try-except to catch file-related errors like FileNotFoundError and ValueError for format issues.

Example:

```
try:
    data = pd.read_csv('data.csv')
except FileNotFoundError:
    print("File not found. Please check the file path.")
except ValueError:
    print("Data format error.")
```

Handling API Errors

When fetching data from APIs, network issues or incorrect endpoints can cause errors.

Solution: Catch exceptions related to network issues or API errors.

Example:

```
import requests

try:
    response = requests.get('https://api.example.com/data')
    response.raise_for_status()
except requests.exceptions.HTTPError as errh:
    print("Http Error:", errh)
except requests.exceptions.ConnectionError as errc:
    print("Error Connecting:", errc)
```

Invalid User Input

AI applications often rely on user input, which can be unpredictable.

Solution: Validate user input and use try-except to handle unexpected or invalid input.

Example:

```
try:
    age = int(input("Enter your age: "))
except ValueError:
    print("Invalid input. Please enter a number.")
```

Error in Data Processing

Operations on data, especially using libraries like NumPy or Pandas, can throw errors due to invalid operations or incompatible data types.

Solution: Implement try-except blocks around data processing operations.

Example:

```
try:
    result = df['column1'] / df['column2']
except ZeroDivisionError:
    print("Division by zero error.")
except KeyError:
    print("Column not found.")
```

Handling Model Training Errors

During model training, there can be errors due to incorrect model parameters, data issues, etc.

Solution: Use try-except to catch and handle these errors, especially when using frameworks like TensorFlow or Scikit-Learn.

Example:

```
from sklearn.ensemble import RandomForestClassifier


try:
    model = RandomForestClassifier(n_estimators='two')
    model.fit(X_train, y_train)
except ValueError as e:
    print("Value Error:", e)
```

Best Practices

1. Be as specific as possible with exception types to avoid catching unintended errors.
2. Consider logging errors instead of just printing them, especially in production environments.
3. Use finally block to ensure necessary cleanup actions are performed, like closing files.
4. Sometimes, it's appropriate to raise exceptions to indicate that something went wrong, especially in custom functions or modules.
5. In complex AI applications, you might define custom exceptions to handle specific error conditions unique to your application.

Summary

In this chapter, we navigated the critical terrain of Python error handling, with a particular emphasis on its use in the development of AI programs. Error handling is more than just a defensive programming practice; it is a critical component in ensuring the robustness and reliability of AI applications. We looked at how to use try-except blocks, Python's primary error-handling mechanism. This entails putting potentially dangerous code in a try block and catching exceptions in an except block. The emphasis was on handling specific error types in order to provide targeted responses to various error conditions, thereby improving program stability and user experience.

We investigated several real-world scenarios in which effective error handling is critical in AI development. This included dealing with errors related to data file operations, such as missing files or format issues, which were handled with the FileNotFoundError and ValueError exceptions. API interactions, which are common in modern AI applications, can fail due to network issues or incorrect endpoints, and we learned how to gracefully handle these situations using requests exceptions. To manage incorrect or unexpected input, prevent crashes, and direct the user towards correct usage, user input, which is often a source of unpredictability, requires careful validation and error handling.

We saw how operations using libraries like Pandas and NumPy might raise errors due to reasons like division by zero or missing columns in the realm of data processing, which is a staple in AI. Demonstrating how to handle these errors not only keeps the application from failing, but also helps with debugging and data quality. Furthermore, AI model training, which is susceptible to errors due to incorrect parameter settings or data issues, necessitates careful error handling. We learned scenarios in which catching and managing exceptions can help to avoid interruptions during the model training and prediction phases.

The emphasis in this chapter was not only on detecting and responding to errors, but also on implementing best practices in error handling. This includes being specific with exception types, logging errors for better debugging and analysis, using the finally block to ensure clean-up actions, and using custom exceptions for specific error conditions. By incorporating these practices, AI developers can create applications that are not only robust in the face of errors, but also provide users with informative feedback, increasing overall user trust and application quality.

CHAPTER 3: DATA AS FUEL FOR AI

Role of Data

Imagine artificial intelligence as a high-end chef. To produce intelligent behavior, artificial intelligence requires data in the same way that a chef needs the appropriate ingredients to create a culinary masterpiece. Aren't you completely captivated by it? Each and every aspect of artificial intelligence, from machine learning to deep learning, is predicated on data. Data like this is essential to the functioning of artificial intelligence systems because it serves as the foundation upon which learning and intelligence are built. Consider the way in which a child acquires knowledge through their experiences; similarly, artificial intelligence algorithms acquire knowledge by processing vast amounts of data, discovering patterns, and making predictions. Artificial intelligence is able to perform tasks such as recognizing speech, translating languages, and even driving cars thanks to the data-driven learning that it possesses. However, having a large quantity of data is not the only thing that matters. The depth, precision, and applicability of this data are the factors that truly enable artificial intelligence. In the same way that we can be led to incorrect conclusions by misinformation, artificial intelligence can be led astray by data of poor quality. Therefore, the importance of collecting data that is both high-quality and relevant is of the utmost importance in the development of AI.

Quality and Diversity of Data

Consider training an AI with skewed data; it's analogous to wearing tinted glasses and believing that is how the entire world appears. This is where AI biases come into play. When an AI model is trained on data that is lacking in diversity, its ability to generalize and make accurate decisions in a variety of real-world scenarios suffers. To be truly effective, an AI trained to recognize faces, for example, requires a diverse dataset representing all ethnicities, ages, and genders. Data diversity ensures that AI models are strong, fair, and unbiased. Furthermore, data quality is critical. Inaccuracies, errors, or poor-quality data can result in faulty AI predictions, similar to constructing a house on shaky ground. Data preprocessing, which entails cleaning, normalizing, and organizing data, is thus an important step in preparing this 'fuel' for AI.

Data in AI Applications

In different AI domains, the role and type of data vary significantly. Consider computer vision, where AI learns from pixels and images to interpret the visual world. Here, the data comprises millions of labeled images. In contrast, in natural language processing (NLP), the AI learns from textual data, requiring a vast corpora of written language to understand and generate human-like text. Each AI application, be it in healthcare, finance, or customer service, demands specific types of data. For instance, AI in healthcare might analyze medical images, patient records, and clinical notes to assist in diagnosis, requiring not just diverse but also highly sensitive and accurate data. The nature of data in AI is thus multifaceted, and its management, from collection to processing, plays a critical role in the success of AI applications.

Future Landscape of Data

In the future, the explosion of data sources, particularly with the introduction of IoT and the growing digital footprint of human activities, presents both challenges and opportunities for AI. The sheer volume and variety of data from which AI can learn is mind-boggling. However, this brings to light the issues of data privacy, security, and ethical use. It will be critical to navigate this landscape responsibly, where data is not only used to power AI but also respected for its privacy and ethical implications. The future of AI is inextricably linked to how we manage this wealth of data, balancing the need for advanced AI capabilities with the need for responsible data stewardship.

The relationship between data and AI is an enthralling dance in which each step of data management influences the AI result. Keeping this intricate relationship in mind as we progress will be critical in realizing AI's full potential.

Data Collection for AI

In order to develop artificial intelligence systems such as our coffee preference prediction app, we discover a wide variety of methods by which data can be collected. Data is comparable to a treasure trove in the field of artificial intelligence, and the manner in which it is collected is just as varied as the data itself. Together, we will go through these different approaches and see how they can be applied to our app.

Traditional Data Collection Methods

Surveys and Questionnaires

These are structured tools for collecting data directly from individuals. They can be conducted online, in-person, or over the phone. You can use surveys to gather information about customers' coffee preferences, frequency of consumption, favorite flavors, and more. This direct approach can provide valuable insights into consumer behavior and preferences.

Observational Data Collection

This involves recording behaviors or occurrences in their natural setting. It can be done manually or through automated systems like CCTV. By observing customer choices and behaviors in a coffee shop, you can gather data on popular products, peak times, customer demographics, etc. This method offers real-world insights that customers might not consciously report in surveys.

Digital Data Collection Methods

Web Scraping

This technique involves extracting data from websites. It's usually done programmatically to gather large amounts of data quickly. Web scraping can be used to collect data from coffee forums, review sites, and online coffee retailers to understand broader market trends, preferences, and customer feedback.

Transactional Data Tracking

This method captures data from transactions, often automatically. In e-commerce, for instance, every purchase, cart addition, or view is recorded. Implementing a system to track all purchases, including the type of coffee, add-ons, and time of purchase, can provide a wealth of data for understanding purchasing patterns and preferences.

Advanced Data Collection Techniques

Social Media Analytics

This involves analyzing data from social media platforms to understand public opinion, trends, and behaviors. By analyzing social media posts, likes, and comments related to coffee, you can gain insights into popular trends, seasonal preferences, and the public perception of different coffee brands or types.

IoT and Sensor Data

The Internet of Things (IoT) allows for the collection of data from interconnected devices. Sensors can provide real-time data on various parameters. IoT devices in coffee machines could collect data on usage patterns, maintenance needs, and customer preferences. Sensors could track how long customers stay, how they interact with the coffee machine, and even environmental factors like temperature and humidity.

The collected data needs to be integrated into a cohesive system for analysis. For our coffee app, this might mean combining survey data with transactional and observational data to create a comprehensive view of customer preferences. Machine learning models can then analyze this integrated data to predict trends, personalized recommendations, and enhance customer experiences. AI thrives on continuous data flow. The more data the coffee app gathers over time, the better it becomes at predicting preferences, adapting to trends, and understanding customer behavior. This continuous learning loop is what makes an AI system like our coffee app not just functional but increasingly sophisticated and attuned to its users.

Leveraging a mix of these methods can provide a rich dataset that reflects both the nuanced preferences of individual customers and broader market trends. The key is to balance the richness of data with ethical considerations, ensuring that the data is not only useful but also responsibly and transparently collected.

Automated Data Collection

Automated data collection is like setting up a self-sustaining garden – once you've planted the seeds and installed a watering system, it largely takes care of itself, growing and flourishing over time. Our goal is to create a system that continuously gathers data about customer preferences and interactions with the coffee app. This system should be capable of capturing a variety of data types, such as transactional data, user input, and perhaps even real-time data from IoT-enabled coffee machines.

Implementing Automated Data Collection

We will break this down into several components, each focusing on a different aspect of data collection. Remember, in a real-world scenario, you'd need to integrate this with your existing infrastructure, like your app backend, database, and possibly IoT devices. Following are the components:

Transactional Data Collection

Capture data every time a customer makes a purchase. Each transaction (e.g., a coffee purchase) triggers a data capture event. Data like the type of coffee, add-ons, time of purchase, and user ID are recorded.

Imagine this as a function in your app's backend (pseudo-code for demonstration):

```
def record_transaction(user_id, coffee_type, addons, purchase_time):
    # This function would interact with your database
    data = {
        "user_id": user_id,
        "coffee_type": coffee_type,
        "addons": addons,
        "purchase_time": purchase_time
    }
    database.save(data)
```

User Preferences and Feedback

Collect data on user preferences and feedback. After a purchase or at regular intervals, prompt users to provide feedback or update preferences. This can be integrated into the app as a feedback form or preference settings.

A function to handle user feedback submissions could look like this:

```
def submit_feedback(user_id, feedback, rating):
    feedback_data = {
        "user_id": user_id,
        "feedback": feedback,
        "rating": rating
    }
    database.save(feedback_data)
```

Real-Time Data from IoT Coffee Machines

If you have IoT-enabled coffee machines, collect data like machine usage patterns, maintenance needs, etc. Coffee machines send data to a centralized server or cloud platform. Data could include machine usage stats, maintenance alerts, and customer interactions.

This is more about the setup on the IoT device side, but the server-side might have a function like:

```
def receive_machine_data(machine_id, usage_data):
    # Data received from IoT coffee machines
    iot_data = {
        "machine_id": machine_id,
        "usage_data": usage_data
    }
    database.save(iot_data)
```

Let us envision a day in the life of our coffee app with automated data collection:

1. Morning Rush: As customers order their morning coffee, transactional data is collected in real-time. The app records what types of coffee are popular during different times of the day.
2. Feedback Loop: After their purchase, customers are prompted to rate their coffee and provide feedback, which is also recorded.
3. IoT Insights: IoT-enabled coffee machines send data about their usage, helping to track which machines are busiest and when maintenance might be needed.

This system becomes the bedrock upon which the app can provide personalized experiences, efficient service, and stay ahead in the market by understanding and predicting customer needs and preferences.

Understanding Data Cleaning

Data cleaning is often likened to preparing the ingredients before cooking; it's about making sure that the data we feed into our AI models is of the highest quality, free from impurities that could skew our results.

Data is often messy – it can be incomplete, inconsistent, or contain errors. Unprocessed raw data may lead to misleading AI predictions and analyses. Data cleaning is the process of fixing or removing incorrect, corrupted, incorrectly formatted, duplicate, or incomplete data within a dataset.

Steps in Data Cleaning

- Identifying Anomalies: Detecting errors or inconsistencies in the data.
- Dealing with Missing Data: Handling null or missing values.
- Data Transformation: Standardizing and normalizing data.
- Removing Duplicates: Identifying and deleting repeated data points.
- Error Correction: Fixing or removing data anomalies and errors.

If we assume that our coffee app has been collecting a variety of data, such as transaction records, customer feedback, data from Internet of Things machines, and so on, so be it. The data needs to be cleaned up at this point.

Handling Missing Values

Some customer feedback entries are missing ratings or comments.

Solution: Replace missing values with a substitute, like the mean or median of that column. If the missing data is significant, consider removing those entries.

Example:

```
# Assuming 'df' is our DataFrame
# Impute missing ratings with the median
df['rating'].fillna(df['rating'].median(), inplace=True)
```

```
# Drop rows where feedback is missing
df.dropna(subset=['feedback'], inplace=True)
```

Correcting Inconsistencies

The format of timestamps or product names is inconsistent.

Solution: Convert all entries into a consistent format.

Example:

```
# Standardizing timestamp format
df['timestamp'] = pd.to_datetime(df['timestamp'])

# Standardizing product names to lowercase
df['product'] = df['product'].str.lower()
```

Removing Duplicates

The dataset has duplicate entries due to a glitch in data collection.

Solution: Identifying and removing duplicate records.

Example:

```
# Dropping duplicate rows
df.drop_duplicates(inplace=True)
```

Dealing with Outliers

Outlier values in transaction amounts or quantities that don't make sense (e.g., extremely high values).

Solution: Use statistical methods to identify and handle outliers.

Example:

```
# Identifying outliers using IQR
Q1 = df['quantity'].quantile(0.25)
Q3 = df['quantity'].quantile(0.75)
IQR = Q3 - Q1
df = df[~((df['quantity'] < (Q1 - 1.5 * IQR)) |(df['quantity'] > (Q3 + 1.5 * IQR)))]
```

Error Correction

Data entry errors in customer or machine IDs.

Solution: Cross-reference IDs with a master list and correct or remove invalid entries.

Example:

```
# Validating customer IDs
valid_ids = get_valid_customer_ids() # Assume this function gets valid IDs
df['customer_id'] = df['customer_id'].apply(lambda x: x if x in valid_ids else np.nan)
df.dropna(subset=['customer_id'], inplace=True)
```

Data Transformation

Data is in different scales or formats that are not suitable for analysis.

Solution: Normalize data scales and encode categorical variables.

Example:

```
# Normalizing a column
df['quantity'] = (df['quantity'] - df['quantity'].mean()) / df['quantity'].std()

# Encoding categorical variables
df = pd.get_dummies(df, columns=['product'])
```

More accurate insights into customer preferences, more efficient inventory management, and improved forecasting of future trends are all outcomes that can be achieved through the utilization of clean data. When the data has been cleaned, it provides a solid foundation upon which the artificial intelligence models of the app can be constructed and trained. By devoting the necessary amount of time and resources to the process of data cleaning, we have laid the groundwork for an artificial intelligence system that is not only dependable but also efficient, with the ability to provide individualized experiences and make predictions based on accurate information.

Preprocessing Methods

If data cleaning is about ensuring the quality of your data, preprocessing is about transforming and fine-tuning that data to make it ready for your AI models. It's an essential step in the AI development pipeline.

Purpose of Data Preprocessing

The purpose of data preprocessing in AI and machine learning is multifaceted, primarily aimed at enhancing model performance. Raw data typically comes in formats that aren't immediately suitable for input into AI models. Preprocessing is the process of transforming this raw data into a format that is more digestible for these models, thereby improving their accuracy and efficiency. An integral part of this process is feature engineering, which involves creating new, more informative features from the existing data. This step can significantly enhance the model's learning capabilities and its accuracy in making predictions.

Another crucial aspect of preprocessing is normalization and scaling. AI models, especially neural networks, often yield better results when the data is on a similar scale. Preprocessing includes various techniques to scale and normalize data, ensuring that all input features contribute equally to the model's performance. Additionally, handling categorical data is a key part of preprocessing. Many machine learning models require inputs to be numerical, so categorical data, such as product names, must be converted into a numerical format. This conversion is essential for the model to process and learn from such data effectively.

Methods of Data Preprocessing

Normalization and Standardization

- Normalization: Adjusts the scale of your data so that it fits within a specific range, typically 0 to 1.
- Standardization: Transforms data to have a mean of zero and a standard deviation of one. It's about centering the distribution on the data.

Encoding Categorical Variables

- One-Hot Encoding: Converts categorical variables into a form that could be provided to

ML algorithms to do a better job in prediction.

- Label Encoding: Each category is assigned a unique integer based on alphabetical ordering.

Feature Engineering

Feature engineering plays a critical role in enhancing the performance of machine learning models. It involves the creative process of constructing new features from the existing dataset to improve the model's ability to recognize patterns and make accurate predictions. This step can involve various techniques, such as aggregating data into new combinations, extracting parts of a date-time stamp (like the day of the week), or creating interaction features that combine two or more variables. The goal is to provide the model with additional, meaningful input that can lead to more nuanced and informed decision-making.

Handling Missing Values

Dealing with missing values is an essential aspect of data preprocessing. Missing data can significantly impact the quality of predictions made by a model. Techniques for handling missing values include imputation, where missing values are replaced with substituted values (like the mean or median of the column), and the removal of rows or columns that contain missing values, which is often considered when the proportion of missing data is high and imputation might introduce significant bias. The choice of method depends on the nature of the data and the missing values, as well as the type of model being used.

Data Transformation

Data transformation is crucial for modifying and standardizing the original data into a format that can be effectively utilized by machine learning algorithms. This includes log transformation and box-cox transformation, which are techniques used to stabilize variance across data that may have non-constant variance (heteroscedasticity). These transformations are particularly useful when dealing with skewed data, as they can help to normalize the distribution of features. Additionally, other transformations like scaling (e.g., Min-Max scaling or Z-score normalization) ensure that all features contribute equally to the model's performance and prevent features with larger scales from dominating those with smaller scales.

Data Preprocessing on Coffee App Data

Now we will preprocess the sample dataset of our coffee app, which includes daily transactions, types of coffee sold, and customer feedback.

Sample Dataset:

```
data = {
```

```
    'Day': ['Mon', 'Tue', 'Wed', 'Thu', 'Fri', 'Sat', 'Sun'],
    'Espresso': [75, 50, 60, 80, 90, 120, 110],
    'Latte': [200, 180, 190, 210, 230, 300, 280],
    'Cappuccino': [150, 130, 140, 170, 180, 250, 220],
    'Customer_Feedback': ['Good', 'Good', 'Average', 'Poor', 'Good', 'Excellent', 'Average']
}

df = pd.DataFrame(data)
```

Encoding Categorical Data

Convert 'Customer_Feedback' into a numerical format for analysis.

```
feedback_mapping = {'Poor': 1, 'Average': 2, 'Good': 3, 'Excellent': 4}
df['Customer_Feedback_Encoded'] = df['Customer_Feedback'].map(feedback_mapping)
```

Normalization

Normalize the sales data to ensure they are on the same scale.

```
from sklearn.preprocessing import MinMaxScaler

scaler = MinMaxScaler()
df[['Espresso', 'Latte', 'Cappuccino']] = scaler.fit_transform(df[['Espresso', 'Latte', 'Cappuccino']])
```

Handling Missing Values

Suppose some values in 'Cappuccino' are missing. We need to address this.

```
# Assuming some NaN values in 'Cappuccino'
df['Cappuccino'].fillna(df['Cappuccino'].mean(), inplace=True)
```

Feature Engineering

Create a new feature that could be useful for prediction, like total sales.

```
df['Total_Sales'] = df['Espresso'] + df['Latte'] + df['Cappuccino']
```

Data Transformation

Stabilize variance across the dataset.

```
df['Total_Sales_Log'] = np.log(df['Total_Sales'] + 1)
```

Once preprocessing is complete, the data is now ready to be used in training our AI models. After going through the meticulous processes of data cleaning and preprocessing, our dataset for the coffee preference prediction app has been transformed significantly, making it more suitable for AI analysis and modeling.

Following is how the dataset for our prediction model looks after the cleaning and preprocessing stages:

1. Days of the Week (Day): This column remains unchanged as it's already in a suitable format.

2. Normalized Sales Data (Espresso, Latte, Cappuccino): Each of these columns has been normalized to scale the sales data between 0 and 1. This normalization helps in equalizing the influence of each coffee type in the dataset and makes the data more suitable for AI models that are sensitive to the scale of input data.

3. Customer Feedback (Customer_Feedback): Originally textual data, it has been encoded into numerical values for better processing by AI models. The encoding follows: 'Poor' as 1, 'Average' as 2, 'Good' as 3, and 'Excellent' as 4.

4. Customer Feedback Encoded (Customer_Feedback_Encoded): This new column represents the numerical encoding of the customer feedback.

5. Total Sales (Total_Sales): A new feature created through feature engineering, representing the sum of normalized sales of Espresso, Latte, and Cappuccino. This column provides a consolidated view of total sales for each day.

6. Log Transformed Total Sales (Total_Sales_Log): We applied a log transformation to the total sales data to stabilize variance and handle skewness. This transformation makes the data more suitable for models that assume normality of the input data.

The dataset is now refined and structured, making it more conducive for training sophisticated AI models.

Exploratory Data Analysis

EDA (Exploratory Data Analysis) is a critical first step in AI and machine learning projects. It entails analyzing and researching data sets in order to identify patterns, anomalies, trends, and relationships between variables. EDA is important in AI because it informs the choice of appropriate models and features, directs data preprocessing strategies, and aids in hypothesis generation. Statistical summaries, visualization tools such as scatter plots and histograms, and correlation analysis are all used in EDA. AI practitioners can make informed decisions on how to proceed with model development and training by understanding the underlying structure and characteristics of the data, ultimately leading to more effective and efficient AI solutions.

Importance of EDA

- EDA helps in getting familiar with the data's structure, distribution, and relationships between variables. It's about asking questions, being curious, and exploring the data to understand its nuances and intricacies.

- Detecting patterns, trends, and correlations between variables can provide valuable insights. Spotting anomalies or outliers that could indicate errors or important, rare events.

- EDA can direct the choice of appropriate models and features for machine learning. It helps in validating assumptions and choosing parameters for model training.

- EDA often reveals the need for further data cleaning or transformation. It lays the groundwork for preprocessing steps like normalization, encoding, and handling missing values.

Performing EDA

We should use EDA to analyze our preprocessed coffee app dataset. Our dataset contains sales data for various coffee types, customer feedback, and engineered features such as total sales and log-transformed total sales.

Following are some EDA operations on our dataset that comes to my mind:

Visualizing Sales Distribution

```
df[['Espresso', 'Latte', 'Cappuccino']].plot(kind='box', figsize=(10, 6))
```

```
plt.title("Distribution of Coffee Sales")
plt.ylabel("Normalized Sales")
plt.show()
```

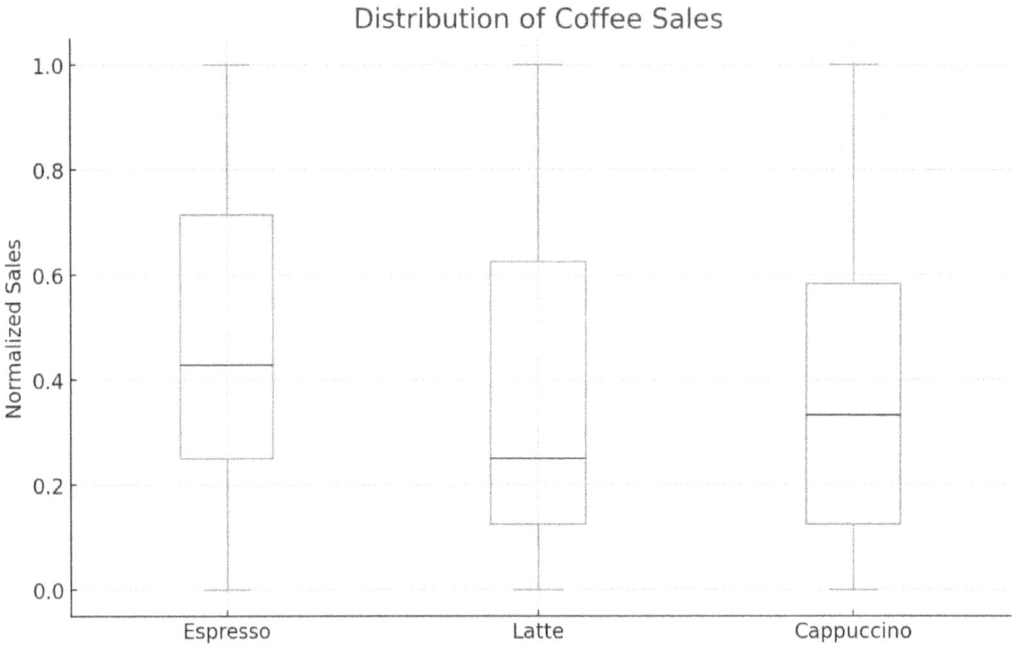

Fig 3.1 Box Plot of Coffee Sales

The box plot illustrates the distribution of normalized sales for Espresso, Latte, and Cappuccino. It's a clear way to observe the range and variation in sales for each type of coffee, including median values and potential outliers.

Correlation Heatmap

```
corr = df[['Espresso', 'Latte', 'Cappuccino', "Total_Sales_Log']].corr()
sns.heatmap(corr, annot=True, cmap='Blues')
plt.title("Correlation Heatmap")
plt.show()
```

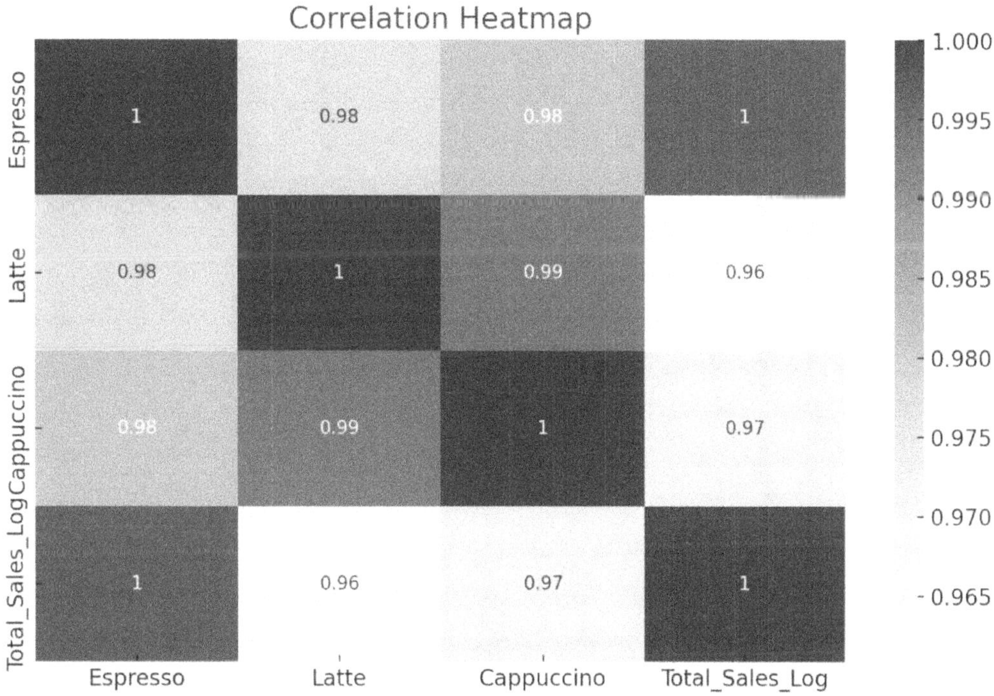

Fig 3.2 Correlation Heatmap

This heatmap shows the correlation between different coffee types and the log-transformed total sales. The annotated values provide a quantifiable measure of how strongly the sales of one type correlate with others, which can be crucial for understanding customer purchasing patterns.

Sales Trends Over the Week

```
df.groupby('Day')['Total_Sales_Log'].sum().plot(kind='line', marker='o')
plt.title("Total Sales Log Over the Week")
plt.xlabel("Day")
plt.ylabel("Log of Total Sales")
plt.show()
```

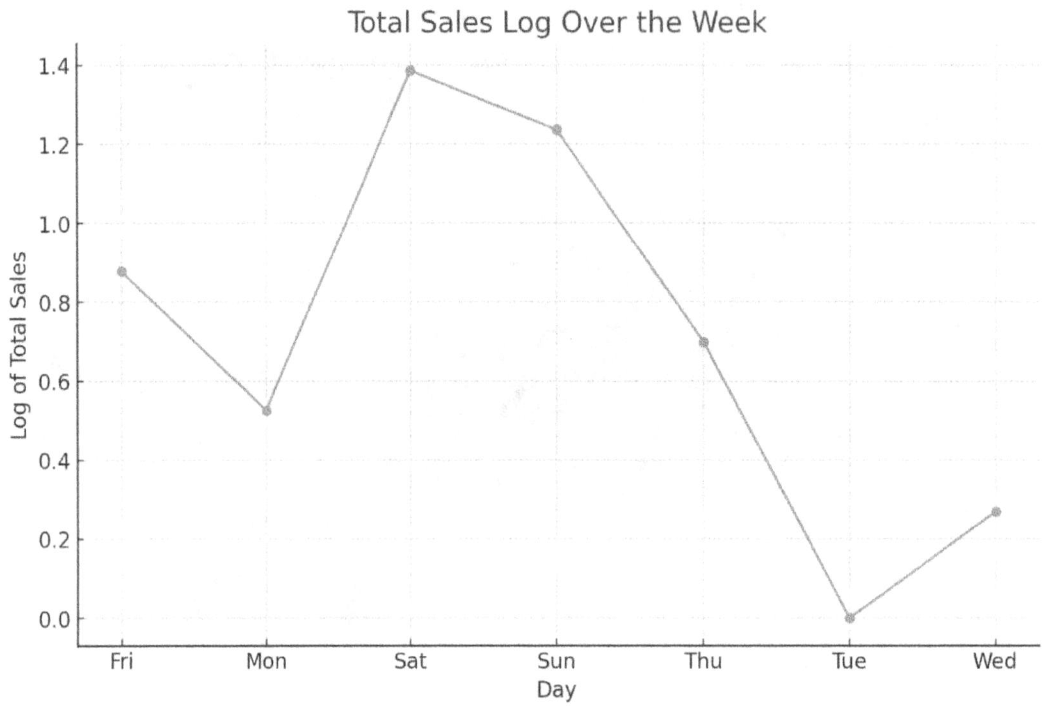

Fig 3.3 Line Graph on Weekly Sales

The line graph displays the logarithm of total sales over the week. It provides a temporal view of sales, highlighting trends and patterns on specific days. Such insights can be valuable for inventory management and promotional planning.

Feedback and Sales Relationship

```
sns.barplot(x='Customer_Feedback', y='Total_Sales', data=df)
plt.title("Customer Feedback vs. Total Sales")
plt.show()
```

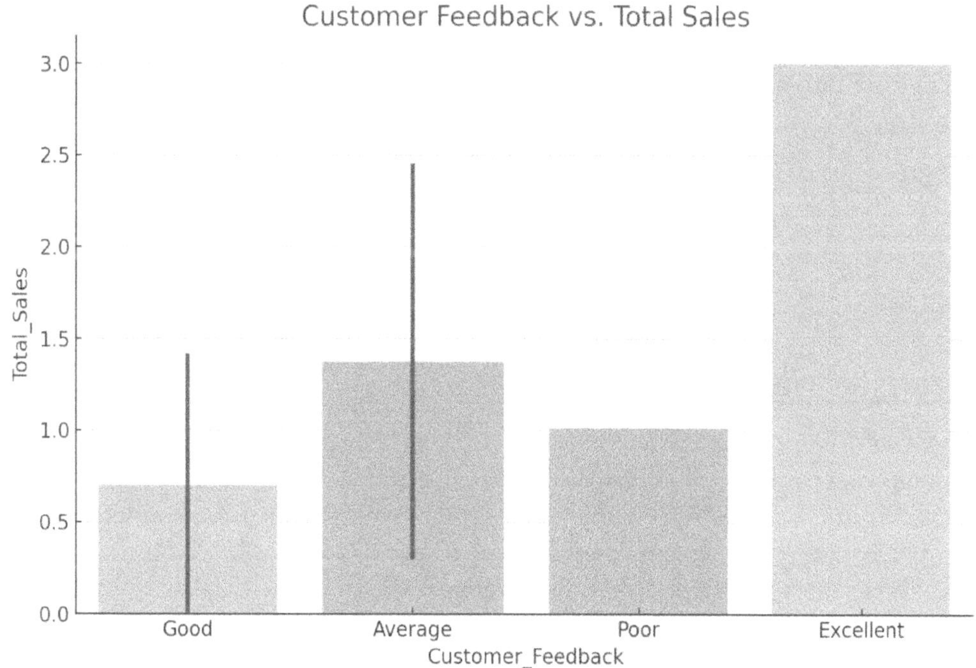

Fig 3.4 Feeback-Sales Relationship Bar Plot

This bar plot examines the relationship between customer feedback and total sales. It offers a visual representation of how different feedback categories (Poor, Average, Good, Excellent) relate to the overall sales, which can be pivotal in understanding customer satisfaction and its impact on business.

We've seen how sales vary across different coffee types and days of the week, and how customer feedback relates to sales. This process has not only deepened our understanding of the data but also potentially highlighted areas for further investigation, such as the impact of specific days on sales, or how customer feedback might influence purchase patterns. EDA is quite an iterative and exploratory journey, a dialogue with the data that directs us towards more informed, data-driven decisions in the AI model-building process.

Data Transformation

Data transformation is a critical process in preparing your data for effective AI modeling. Think of it as a chef preparing ingredients before cooking a meal. Just as a chef chops, seasons, or marinades ingredients to enhance the dish's flavor, data transformation involves modifying your data to improve the performance and accuracy of your AI models.

Firstly, AI models often require data in a specific format or distribution to work effectively. Data transformation ensures that the data meets these requirements, leading to more accurate and efficient models. Also, data collected from different sources can vary in formats and scales. Transforming data into a standard format is essential for consistent analysis and modeling. Some AI models struggle with complex, high-dimensional data. Transforming data can reduce its complexity, making it more manageable for these models.

It is worth noting that AI models generally perform better on data that is evenly distributed. Transforming skewed data can improve model performance, especially in regression and classification tasks.

Data Transformation Techniques

Normalization

This technique scales numerical data to a fixed range, typically between 0 and 1. The process involves rescaling the features within this range. It's particularly useful when working with data that varies in scale and for algorithms that do not presuppose a specific distribution of data, such as K-Nearest Neighbors and Artificial Neural Networks.

Standardization

The goal is to center the data around zero (mean) while ensuring a unit standard deviation. This is achieved by subtracting the mean from each data point and then dividing by the standard deviation. Standardization is crucial for algorithms that assume a Gaussian (normal) distribution of data, such as Logistic Regression, Linear Discriminant Analysis, and Gaussian Naive Bayes.

Log Transformation

This technique is aimed at reducing data skewness, especially in datasets with long tails. It involves applying the natural logarithm or logarithm of base 10 to each data point. It's particularly useful for handling exponential and multiplicative data, often seen in financial modeling.

Box-Cox Transformation

This transformation modifies data to follow a normal distribution. It determines an appropriate power transformation to achieve this normality. It's typically used when the data exhibits heteroscedasticity, meaning the variance is non-constant.

Feature Encoding

This process converts categorical data into a numerical format, essential for algorithms requiring numerical input. There are two primary types:

1. One-Hot Encoding, which creates a binary column for each category.
2. Label Encoding, which assigns a unique integer to each category.

Binning

This technique groups numeric data into categories or bins, effectively converting numeric data into categorical data. Binning helps in reducing the impact of minor observation errors and addresses real-world data inaccuracies.

Discretization

It involves converting continuous data into discrete bins or intervals, each representing a category. Discretization is often utilized in machine learning, especially for classification tasks in decision trees.

Each of the techniques listed above serves a specific purpose and is chosen based on the nature of the data and the needs of the analysis or machine learning algorithm in use. Data transformation is analogous to preparing the stage for the main actors (AI algorithms). Each transformation technique, whether scaling, normalizing, encoding, or reducing dimensionality, has a distinct role and importance, depending on the type of data and the specific requirements of the AI model. Just as a well-prepared ingredient can elevate a dish, well-transformed data can distinguish a mediocre AI model from a highly effective one.

Feature Engineering

In AI and machine learning, feature engineering is an excellent art. The process is analogous to that of a sculptor chipping away at a block of marble, transforming raw data into features that reveal the hidden beauty of insightful patterns and trends. It entails transforming raw data into features that more accurately represent the underlying problem to the predictive models, which ultimately results in improved accuracy and performance of the models. The process of extracting features from raw data by making use of relevant domain knowledge is referred to as feature engineering. The presence of these features is what makes machine learning algorithms functional, and the ability to effectively engineer features can be the key to unlocking improved model performance.

Importance of Feature Engineering

- Well-engineered features provide a clear and focused lens for AI models to learn from, which can significantly improve their accuracy and performance.

- By transforming data into meaningful features, you can reduce the complexity of the data and thus the model. It helps in simplifying the model, making it faster and more efficient.

- Feature engineering can reveal patterns in the data that might not be immediately apparent, providing deeper insights and more accurate predictions.

- Features created through domain knowledge are often more interpretable, making it easier to understand the model's decisions.

Techniques in Feature Engineering

Feature Creation

Involves creating new features from existing data. This can be as simple as creating a feature that captures the total sales per day or as complex as a feature that encapsulates the seasonality in sales data.

Example: In our coffee app, creating a feature that represents the peak sales time during the day. Suppose you have timestamp data for each transaction. You can engineer features like 'time of the day' or 'day of the week' to capture patterns in customer behavior at different times.

Feature Transformation

Transforms features into a format that is more suitable for modeling. This can include scaling, normalization, or more complex transformations like Box-Cox or Yeo-Johnson transformations.

Example: Transforming sales data into a logarithmic scale to normalize the distribution. Or From transaction history, you could create features that represent a customer's preference for a type of coffee or their average spending per visit.

Feature Extraction

Involves extracting features from datasets, particularly useful in unstructured data like text or images.

Example: Extracting the sentiment from customer reviews using natural language processing.

Feature Encoding

Converts categorical data into numerical format. This is essential because most machine learning algorithms require numerical input.

Example: Encoding types of coffee as numerical values for model input.

Dimensionality Reduction

Techniques like PCA (Principal Component Analysis) are used to reduce the number of features in a dataset while retaining most of the information.

Example: Reducing the number of features in a dataset with many correlated variables.

Summary

We explored the critical process of feature engineering in AI app development in this chapter, revealing how it acts as a transformative bridge between raw data and insightful, effective machine learning models. At its core, feature engineering is about transforming data in novel ways to significantly improve the performance and accuracy of AI models. It's analogous to a craftsman shaping raw materials into intricate parts of complicated machinery. We investigated techniques such as feature creation, transformation, extraction, encoding, and dimensionality reduction, each of which served a distinct purpose in shaping the data into a more useful form for AI models.

Feature creation and transformation emerged as critical techniques, in which new features are created from existing data and existing features are transformed to better suit AI models. In our coffee app scenario, for example, we learned developing time-based features based on transaction timestamps that could reveal customer behavior patterns at different times of the day or week. Similarly, transforming sales data into logarithmic scales was emphasized in order to normalize distributions and make the data more palatable for certain types of AI models. These techniques emphasize the significance of not only the quantity, but also the quality and format of data fed into AI systems.

Furthermore, we emphasized the importance of feature extraction and encoding when dealing with unstructured data such as text and images, which is a common challenge in AI projects. Extraction of sentiment from customer feedback, for example, is a natural language processing technique that converts qualitative data into quantifiable scores that an AI model can interpret and learn from. This aspect of feature engineering opens up a slew of AI possibilities, allowing models to delve into more complex, human-like data comprehension.

The chapter also demonstrated how feature engineering is a cog in the larger wheel of AI app development, rather than a stand-alone process. It is intertwined with later stages such as model selection, training, evaluation, and deployment. The iterative nature of feature engineering, its relationship to model performance, and its role in model selection and evaluation were emphasized, emphasizing its dynamic nature in the AI modeling process.

CHAPTER 4: MACHINE LEARNING FOUNDATIONS

Machine Learning Overview

Do you have an interest in learning more about how machine learning (ML) has developed within the domain of artificial intelligence (AI)? Consider artificial intelligence to be a massive tree. The field of machine learning is one of its most active subfields, and it is actively expanding and expanding into new and exciting directions. In the beginning, artificial intelligence was primarily concerned with rule-based systems, which were computers that were programmed to react to particular inputs with particular outputs. You could compare it to following a recipe. But there was a catch: these systems were incapable of learning or adapting beyond the programming that they were initially programmed with.

The advent of machine learning proved to be a game-changer. The paradigm shifted from rule-based systems to algorithms that could learn from data, make predictions, and improve over time. This was considered a significant advancement. Comparatively speaking, this was more like instructing someone on how to cook than simply following a recipe. The capability of machine learning to learn from data, recognize patterns, and make decisions with minimal intervention from humans represented a significant step forward in the development of intelligent systems.

Machine Learning's Contribution to AI

Machine Learning's contribution to AI is profound. It's like adding a supercharger to an engine. ML has enabled AI to tackle complex problems that were previously thought to be the sole domain of human intelligence. From image and speech recognition to predictive analytics, ML algorithms have been at the forefront, pushing the boundaries of what machines can do.

One of the most exciting aspects of ML in AI is its versatility. It's not just about one type of task or application. You've got different flavors of ML, each suited for different kinds of problems. For instance:

- Supervised Learning: It's like teaching a child with examples. You provide the algorithm with labeled training data, and it learns to predict the output from the input data. It's widely used in applications like fraud detection and customer segmentation.
- Unsupervised Learning: This is more about exploration. Here, the algorithm is given data without explicit instructions on what to do with it. It's used for clustering and association tasks, like market basket analysis or customer segmentation.
- Reinforcement Learning: Think of it as training a pet. The algorithm learns by trial and error to achieve a defined goal. It's used in areas like robotics and gaming, where the algorithm must make a series of decisions.

The Impact of Machine Learning

The impact of ML on AI and technology as a whole is staggering. It has revolutionized how we interact with technology, how businesses operate, and even how we perceive the world. Personal assistants like Siri and Alexa, recommendation systems used by Netflix and Amazon, and self-driving cars are all powered by ML.

Moreover, ML has opened doors to new possibilities in healthcare, finance, and even in tackling social challenges. In healthcare, ML algorithms help diagnose diseases, personalize treatments, and even predict outbreaks. In finance, they're used for risk assessment, algorithmic trading, and fraud detection. The scope is vast and continuously expanding.

Despite its advancements, ML is not without its challenges. There's the issue of data quality – ML models are only as good as the data they're trained on. Then there is the black box problem, where some ML models are not very transparent, making it hard to understand how they arrive at certain decisions. Ethical considerations, particularly in the use of personal data and the potential biases in ML models, are also significant concerns. The integration of ML with other technologies, like IoT and blockchain, is another exciting frontier. The goal is to make ML more efficient, transparent, and accessible, ultimately contributing to an AI landscape that is more intelligent, ethical, and beneficial for humanity.

Supervised Learning Process

Imagine supervised learning as a teaching process. Just like a student learns from a teacher, supervised learning algorithms learn from labeled data. The 'supervised' part comes from the fact that the learning process is supervised by known outputs. It's like teaching someone to distinguish between different types of coffee by showing them several examples of each type.

Data is at the heart of supervised learning. The data used in this process is labeled, meaning it includes both the input (features) and the desired output (label). For our coffee app, imagine we have a dataset of customers' coffee orders (input) and their satisfaction ratings (output).

The process of supervised learning can be visualized through a flow chart:

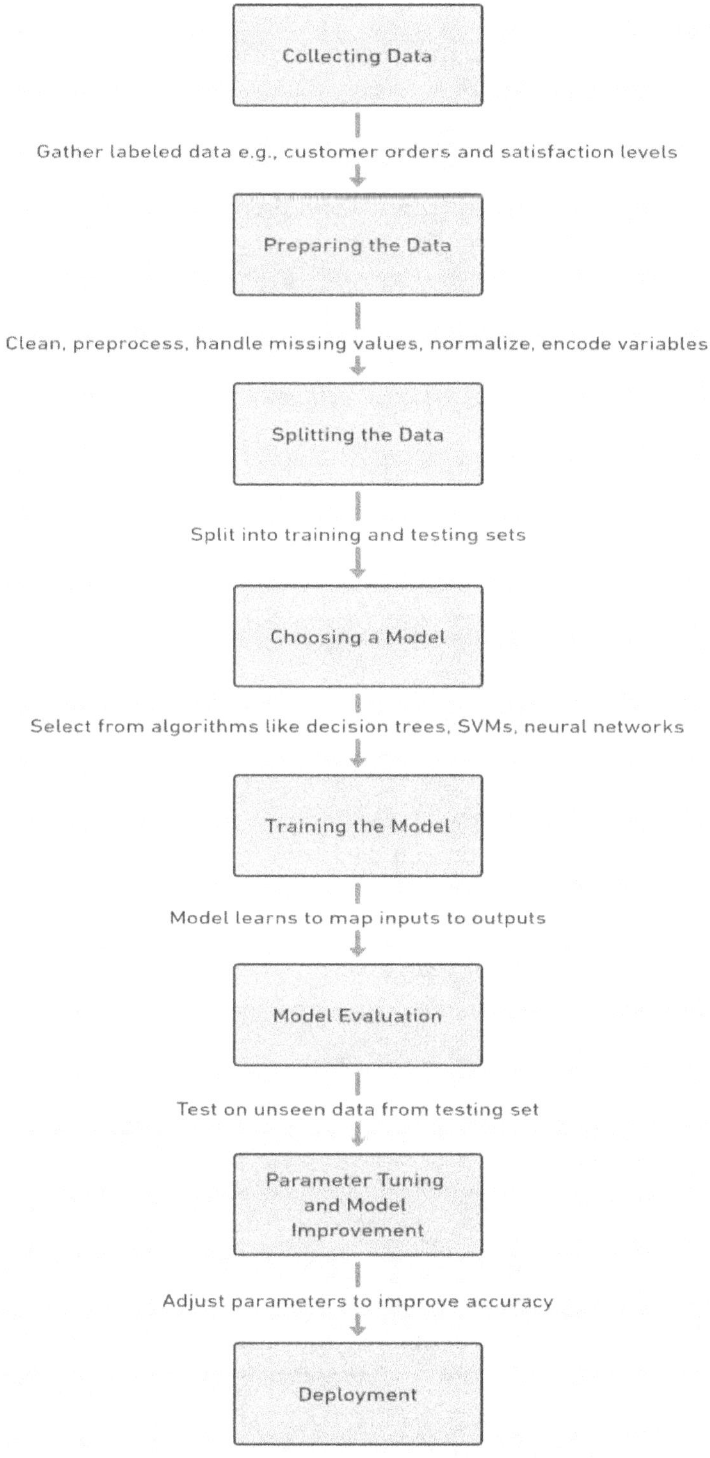

Fig 4.1 Supervised Learning Process Flow

Collecting Data

The first step is gathering labeled data. In our context, this could be historical data of customer orders and their satisfaction levels.

Preparing the Data

Once the data is collected, it needs to be cleaned and preprocessed. This might involve handling missing values, normalizing data, or encoding categorical variables.

Splitting the Data

The data is then split into training and testing sets. The training set is used to teach the model, while the testing set is used to evaluate its performance.

Choosing a Model

There are various algorithms for supervised learning, such as decision trees, support vector machines, or neural networks. The choice depends on the nature of the data and the problem at hand.

Training the Model

The model learns from the training data. It tries to map the input data to the corresponding outputs.

Model Evaluation

After training, the model is tested on unseen data from the testing set. This evaluates how well the model has learned and how it performs on data it hasn't seen before.

Parameter Tuning and Model Improvement

Based on the model's performance, parameters may need to be adjusted to improve accuracy.

Deployment

Once the model performs satisfactorily, it can be deployed in the real world to make predictions or decisions based on new data.

Assume you're working on a feature in our coffee app that predicts customer satisfaction based on their order details. The supervised learning model would be trained using historical order data as well as satisfaction levels recorded. Once trained, this model can predict whether or not a customer will be satisfied with their order before they provide feedback. This forecast could be used to make real-time recommendations or changes to improve customer satisfaction.

Supervised learning is not just a methodology; it's a pathway to making AI systems more intelligent and responsive. It enables AI systems to learn from examples, improve over time, and make decisions or predictions that are aligned with historical patterns. This learning method is particularly powerful in applications where historical data is abundant and well-labeled, allowing for precise and accurate model training.

Exploring Unsupervised Learning

Unsupervised learning, another key facet of machine learning, presents a different yet equally fascinating approach compared to supervised learning. Imagine us delving into a realm where the AI learns without explicit guidance or labeled data. It's like giving someone a bunch of ingredients and letting them explore various combinations and recipes on their own.

Understanding Unsupervised Learning

In unsupervised learning, the AI is given data without any explicit instructions on what to do with it. There are no labels or predefined categories. The algorithm explores the data, searching for patterns or structures on its own. It's like exploring a new city without a map, discovering hidden gems and patterns in an uncharted territory.

Unsupervised learning is crucial for understanding complex data structures where we might not even know what we're looking for. It's instrumental in identifying hidden patterns, segmenting data into clusters, reducing dimensions for easier analysis, and even in data pre-processing for other AI tasks.

Unsupervised Learning Process

The process of unsupervised learning can be visualized through a flow chart:

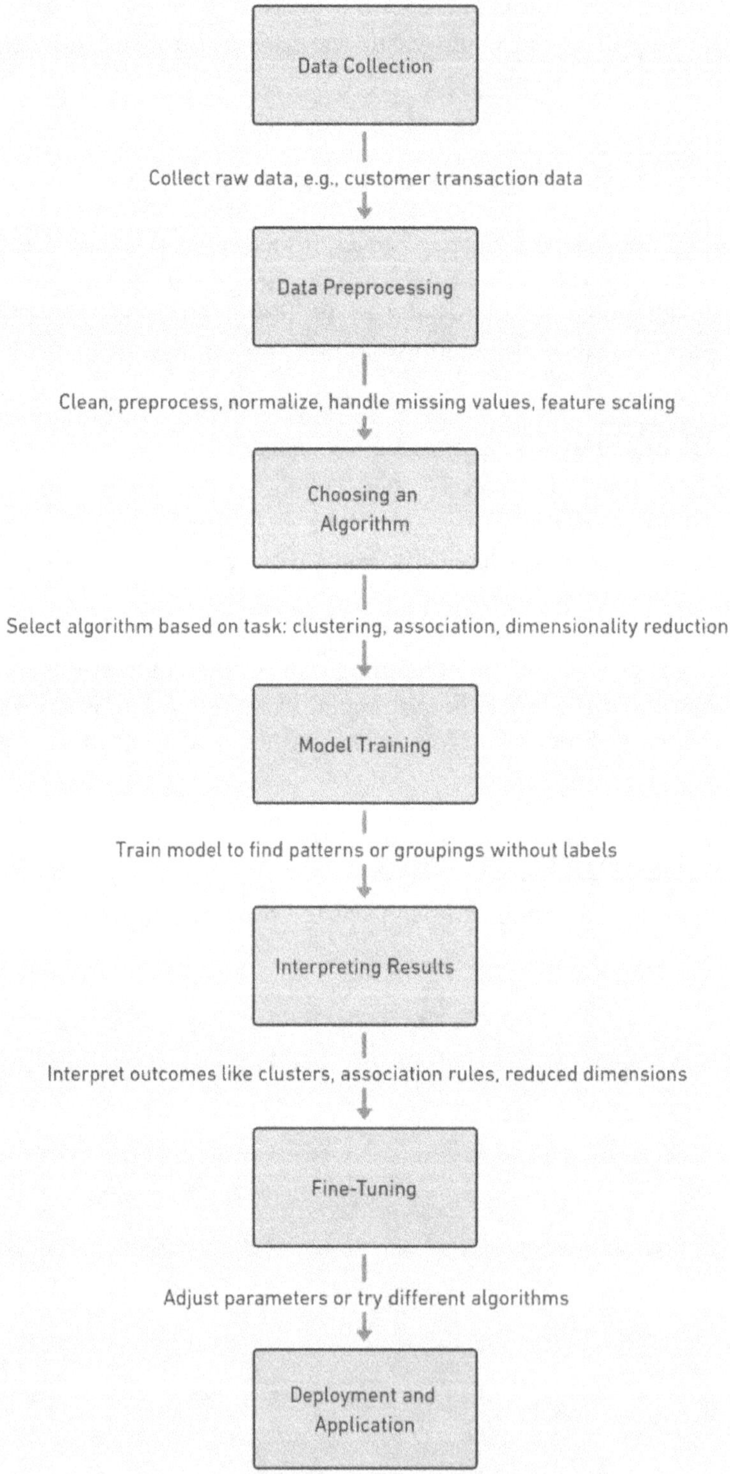

Fig 4.2 Unsupervised Learning Process Flow

Data Collection

The process starts with collecting data. Unlike supervised learning, this data isn't labeled. It's raw data as it is - for instance, customer transaction data without any tags or categories.

Data Preprocessing

Similar to supervised learning, the data needs cleaning and preprocessing. This might include normalization, dealing with missing values, or feature scaling.

Choosing an Algorithm

Depending on the task at hand (like clustering, association, or dimensionality reduction), an appropriate unsupervised learning algorithm is selected. Common algorithms include K-means for clustering, PCA for dimensionality reduction, and Apriori algorithm for association rule learning.

Model Training

The model is trained on the dataset. It tries to find patterns or groupings in the data without any external guidance or labels.

Interpreting Results

The outcome of unsupervised learning can be clusters of data, association rules, or reduced dimensions. These results need to be interpreted to derive meaningful insights.

Fine-Tuning

The model might need fine-tuning to improve its ability to discover structures or patterns in the data. This could involve changing parameters or trying different algorithms.

Deployment and Application

Once satisfactory results are obtained, the model can be deployed. In real-world applications, unsupervised learning models are used for customer segmentation, recommendation systems, anomaly detection, and more.

Unsupervised Learning in Practice

This should be implemented in our coffee application for a real-world scenario. Assume we want to better understand our customer base but do not have predefined customer categories. An unsupervised learning model could analyze purchase patterns, frequency, and preferences to categorize customers. These groups could then be used to customize marketing strategies, offers, and even stock management.

Unsupervised learning is critical for discovering hidden patterns and intrinsic structures in data. It's especially useful in situations where we don't have clear labels, such as exploratory data analysis. This learning paradigm encourages AI autonomy by allowing systems to make sense of data in a more human-like, intuitive manner. It is about discovering the unknowns in datasets and revealing insights that may not be immediately apparent or accessible via supervised methods. This method is essential for comprehending complex datasets, identifying customer segments, detecting anomalies, and simplifying complex data for further analysis.

ML Algorithms Overview

Decision Trees

Decision Trees are a type of supervised learning algorithm used for classification and regression tasks. Picture a tree-like model of decisions, where each branch represents a choice between alternatives, leading to different outcomes or predictions.

Architecture of Decision Trees

- Root Node: Represents the entire dataset, which gets divided into two or more homogeneous sets.
- Splitting: It's the process of dividing a node into two or more sub-nodes based on certain conditions or features.
- Decision Node: When a sub-node splits into further sub-nodes, it's called a decision node.
- Leaf/Terminal Node: Nodes with no further division. They represent the final output or decision.
- Pruning: The process of removing the sub-nodes of a decision node, useful if the branches do not add significant value.
- Branch/Sub-Tree: A subsection of the entire tree.
- Parent and Child Nodes: A node, which is divided into sub-nodes, is called the parent node of the sub-nodes, whereas sub-nodes are the children of the parent node.

How Decision Trees Work?

Decision Trees use a set of binary rules to make decisions, which means each decision only has two outcomes. The decision of how to split at each node is made based on a metric like Gini impurity, information gain, or variance reduction. The algorithm selects the feature and the split point on the feature that provides the best homogeneous sets of populations.

Decision Trees are widely used in areas ranging from customer segmentation, fraud detection, to medical diagnosis.

K-Means Clustering

K-Means is an unsupervised learning algorithm used for clustering. It groups data points into 'k' number of clusters based on feature similarity.

Architecture of K-Means Clustering

- Cluster Centers: These are the central points of each cluster. The number of cluster centers is represented by 'K.'
- Assignment of Data Points: Each data point is assigned to the nearest cluster center.
- Updating Cluster Centers: After all data points are assigned, the cluster centers are recalculated as the mean of all data points in the cluster.
- Iterative Process: The assignment and update steps are repeated iteratively until the positions of the cluster centers stabilize.

How K-Means Clustering Works?

Initially, 'K' cluster centers are chosen randomly. Data points are assigned to the nearest cluster center based on a distance metric, typically Euclidean distance. Once all points are assigned, the positions of the cluster centers are recalculated. The algorithm iterates through the assignment and update steps until the cluster centers no longer move significantly, indicating that the clusters are as homogeneous as possible.

K-Means is used in market segmentation, pattern recognition, image compression, and more.

Sample Program: Applying K-Means Clustering

Following is how the preprocessed coffee preference prediction dataset would be visualized after applying K-Means clustering on the dataset:

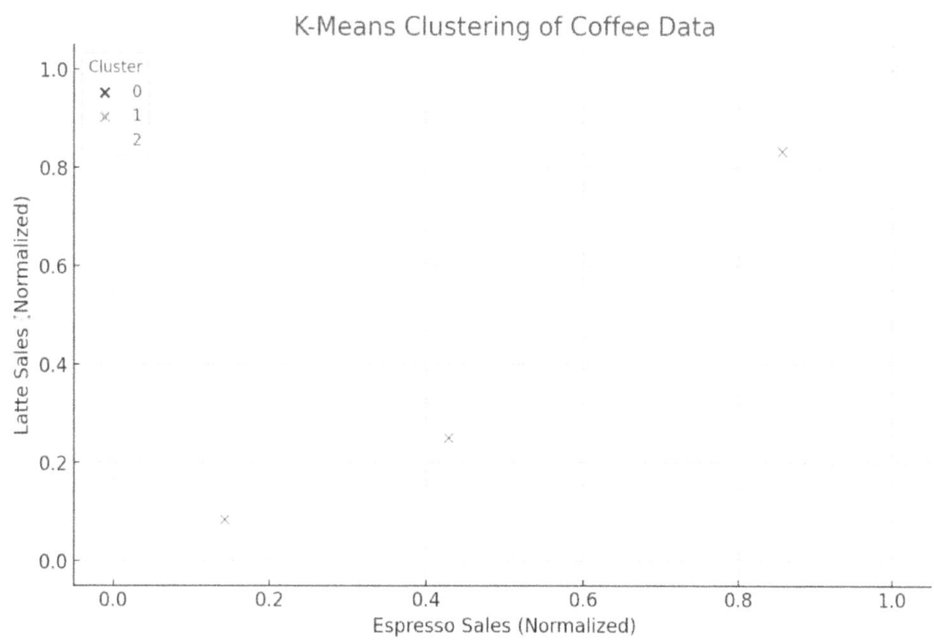

Fig 4.3 Scatter Plot (K-Means Clustering)

In the above, the K-Means algorithm was applied to the dataset with the number of clusters set to 3. This choice of '3' is arbitrary for demonstration purposes, though in a real-world scenario, you might use methods like the elbow method to determine the optimal number of clusters.

The sales data for Espresso, Latte, and Cappuccino were normalized to ensure a uniform scale. This step is crucial as K-Means clustering is sensitive to the scale of the data. The customer feedback, originally categorical, was encoded into numerical values, making it suitable for clustering. A scatter plot was created to visualize the clusters formed by K-Means. Each dot represents a day's data, plotted against normalized Espresso and Latte sales, colored by the cluster it belongs to. The visualization helps in understanding how the algorithm has grouped the days based on sales data and customer feedback. The resulting clusters could represent different customer purchasing behaviors or preferences. For instance, one cluster might represent days with high Espresso sales and positive feedback, while another could represent days with lower sales and varied feedback.

The DataFrame now includes a new column 'Cluster', indicating the cluster each row (day) belongs to. This clustering can provide valuable insights into customer behavior and preferences, assisting in making informed decisions for targeted marketing, inventory management, or even developing new products.

Decision Trees vs. K-Means Clustering

Decision Trees and K-Means Clustering are both effective but distinct approaches to solving machine learning problems. Decision trees stand out for their ease of use, interpretability, and ability to handle both numerical and categorical data. They are especially useful when the decision-making process must be understood or visualized. K-Means, on the other hand, provides a simple and efficient method for segmenting data into clusters, making it ideal for exploratory data analysis and situations where the underlying groupings in the data are unknown. Both algorithms have distinct strengths that make them suitable for a variety of problems in the vast AI landscape.

These algorithms are essential tools in the machine learning toolkit, enabling artificial intelligence systems to analyze, predict, and learn from data in profound ways. Whether it's discovery of hidden patterns with K-Means or making predictions with Decision Trees, these algorithms are essential tools.

Model Training

Understanding Model Training

Model training is the process where an algorithm learns the patterns in the data. For supervised learning, it involves learning the relationship between inputs and outputs from labeled data. In unsupervised learning, like with K-Means, it’s about discovering the inherent structure of the data.

Training involves feeding the algorithm data, allowing it to adjust and improve its parameters (like cluster centroids in K-Means) to optimize a certain objective, such as minimizing the distance between data points and centroids in the case of K-Means.

Effective training is crucial for model accuracy and effectiveness. Poorly trained models can lead to inaccurate predictions or failure to generalize from the training data to new, unseen data.

Training K-Means Model on Coffee Data

In the previous section, we applied K-Means clustering to our normalized coffee sales and customer feedback data. The goal was to group the data into clusters that reflect different purchasing behaviors or preferences.

Training Process

1. Initialization: K-Means starts by initializing 'k' centroids randomly.
2. Assignment Step: Each data point is assigned to the nearest centroid, forming k clusters.
3. Update Step: The centroids are recalculated as the mean of all points in each cluster.
4. Iteration: Steps 2 and 3 are repeated until the centroids stabilize and don't change significantly.

Visualization of Training Process

Visualizing the training process of K-Means involves plotting the data points and centroids at each iteration to see how the clusters evolve.

Sample Program: Visualize Training of K-Means

We will implement and visualize the training process:

We already trained a K-Means model with 3 clusters on our dataset. We then visualize this process. We can plot the data points and centroids for several iterations to see how the clusters evolve.

```
# Visualizing the training process
for i in range(1, 6):  # Consider 5 iterations for demonstration
    kmeans = KMeans(n_clusters=3, random_state=42, n_init=1, max_iter=i)
    df['Cluster'] = kmeans.fit_predict(X)
    centroids = kmeans.cluster_centers_
    plt.figure(figsize=(10, 6))
    sns.scatterplot(x='Espresso', y='Latte', hue='Cluster', data=df, palette='viridis')
```

```
plt.scatter(centroids[:, 0], centroids[:, 1], s=300, c='red', marker='X')  # Centroids
plt.title(f'K-Means Clustering Iteration {i}')
plt.xlabel('Espresso Sales (Normalized)')
plt.ylabel('Latte Sales (Normalized)')
plt.show()
```

Following are the visualizations showing the training process of the K-Means clustering algorithm on our coffee app dataset over five iterations:

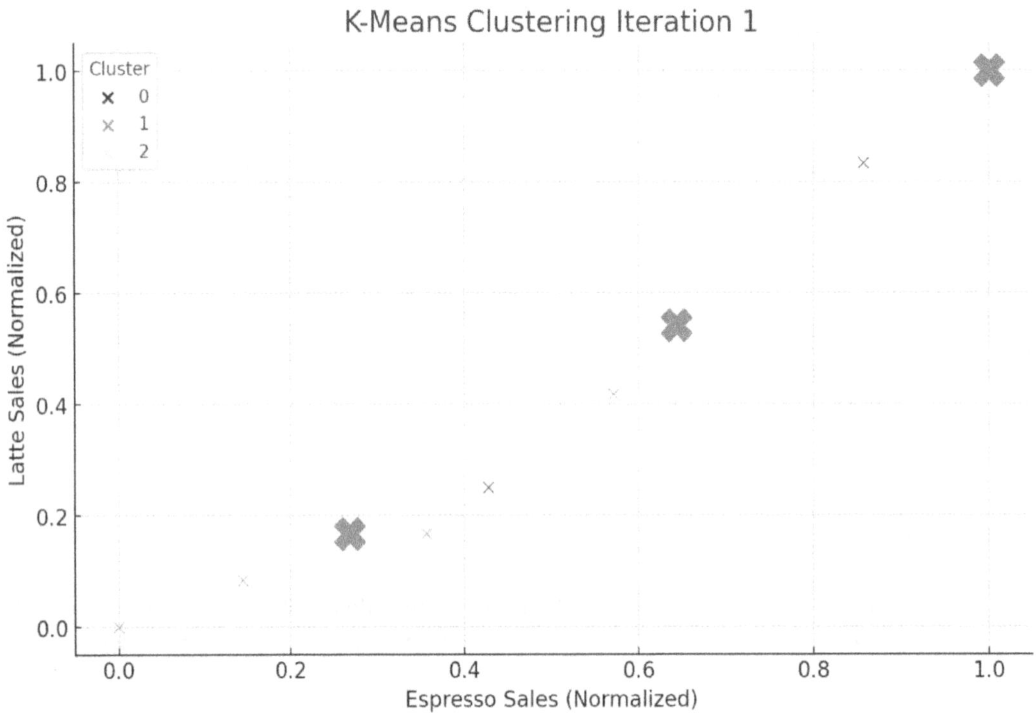

Fig 4.4 Scatter Plot Iteration 1

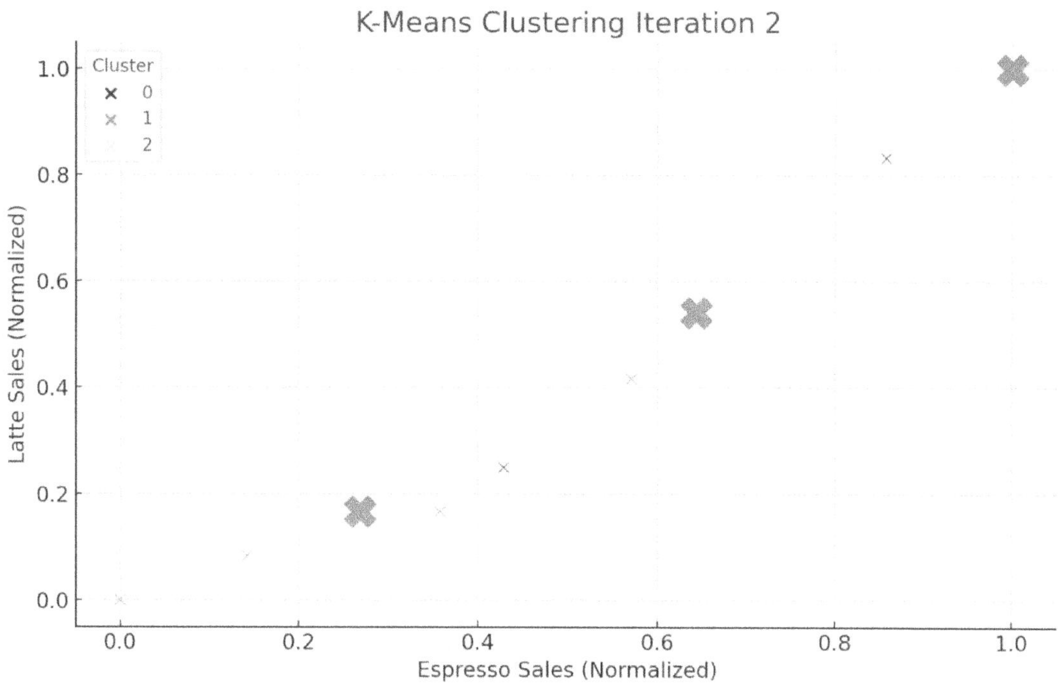

Fig 4.5 Scatter Plot Iteration 2

Fig 4.6 Scatter Plot Iteration 3

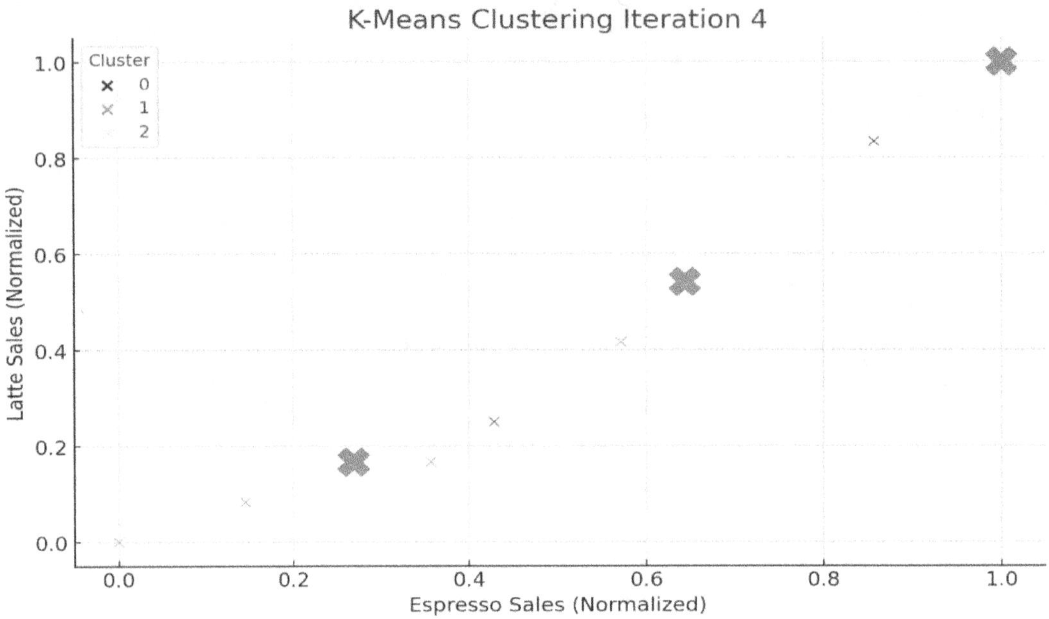

Fig 4.7 Scatter Plot Iteration 4

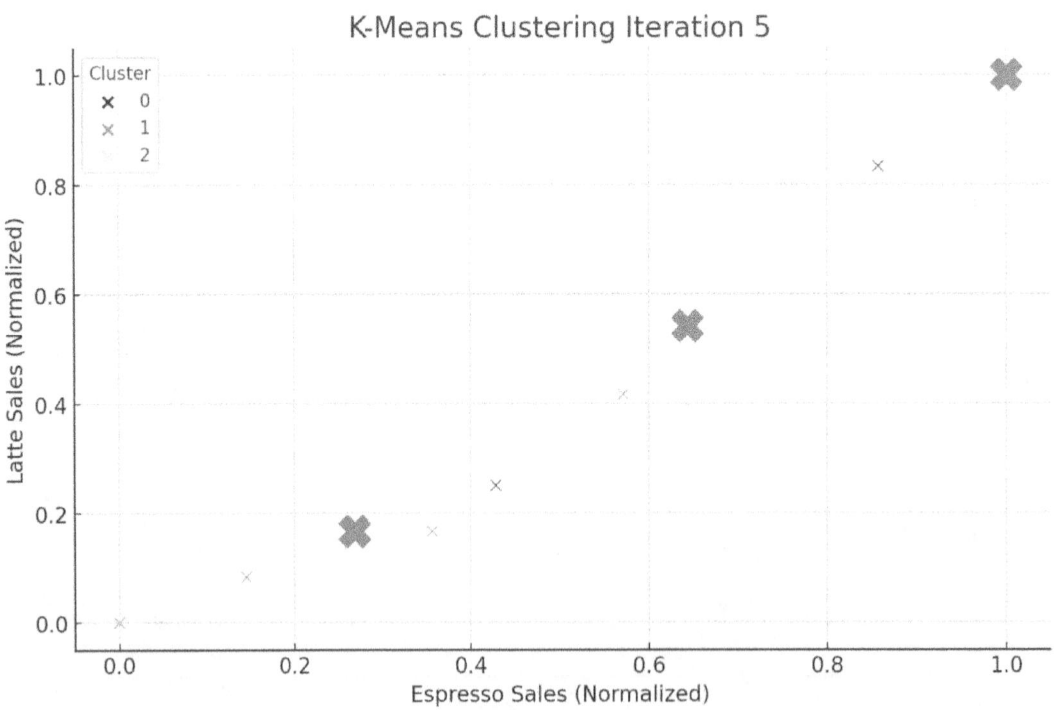

Fig 4.8 Scatter Plot Iteration 5

The scatter plot represents the coffee data points in each of the five iterations, with Espresso and Latte sales on the axes. The points are colored according to the cluster to which they belong in that iteration of the K-Means algorithm. You can see how the clusters change with each iteration. The algorithm reassigns data points to clusters based on the centroids' updated positions. In our case, this may appear to be due to a minor/no change in the dataset.

The centroids of the clusters are represented by the red or (gray) 'X' markers. These centroids shift with each iteration, indicating that the algorithm is recalculating and optimizing their positions to better represent the clusters' centers. The movement of the centroids decreases as the iterations progress, indicating that the algorithm is approaching an optimal solution in which the centroids stabilize, representing the best possible grouping of the data given the number of clusters chosen.

These visualizations effectively demonstrate how K-Means learns the best clustering for the dataset iteratively. By observing these changes, one can learn about the nature of the data and how well it clusters, which is important for understanding customer behaviors and preferences in the context of our coffee app.

Overfitting and Underfitting

Understanding Overfitting

What is Overfitting?

Overfitting is a critical issue in machine learning in which the model learns excessively from the training data, to the point of absorbing its noise and outliers. This is analogous to memorizing a book without understanding the underlying story; the model becomes overly complex, latching onto deceptive patterns in the training data that do not apply to new, unseen data.

Signs of Overfitting

Overfitting symptoms are frequently obvious. For example, the model may be extremely accurate on training data but perform poorly on new or test data. The model has learned the noise and random fluctuations in the training data, mistaking them for meaningful trends rather than understanding the actual underlying patterns.

Preventing Overfitting

Several strategies can be used to avoid overfitting. One method is to simplify the model, either by reducing the number of features it employs or by reducing its overall complexity. Cross-validation is another effective method that involves dividing the training data into several subsets. After that, the model is trained and validated on these various subsets, allowing it to learn more generalized patterns. Regularization techniques such as Lasso or Ridge regression can also be used to keep the model from becoming too complex by penalizing overfitting. Finally, increasing the volume of training data can help because it gives the model a wider range of examples to learn from, reducing the model's tendency to overfit to a limited set of data.

Understanding Underfitting

What is Underfitting?

Underfitting in machine learning is the opposite extreme of model inaccuracy, in which the model is overly simplistic and unable to discern the important patterns in the data. This is analogous to attempting to understand the nuances of a complex story based solely on a brief summary. In these cases, the model's simplicity impedes its learning process, resulting in poor performance not only on unseen data but also on training data.

Signs of Underfitting

The signs of underfitting are simple to identify. The model performs noticeably poorly even on training data, indicating the model's inability to capture the data's complexity and variability. This is frequently due to the model's overly simplistic structure, which lacks the ability to understand or represent the data's intricate relationships.

Preventing Underfitting

Several measures can be implemented to combat underfitting. Increasing the model's complexity is one effective strategy. This can be accomplished by adding more features to the model or by employing more sophisticated and capable modeling techniques. Furthermore, ensuring that the model receives adequate training is critical, as under-trained models frequently underfit. Another critical strategy is feature engineering, which entails improving the quality and relevance of input data. The model receives more informative and nuanced information as the input data is refined, which can aid in capturing the true underlying patterns in the data.

Significance of Overfitting and Underfitting

Both overfitting and underfitting are detrimental to the performance of a model. They impair a model's ability to generalize, which is required for making accurate predictions on new, previously unseen data. To avoid these issues and create a model that not only learns well from training data but also performs well on new data, the model's complexity and simplicity must be balanced.

Overfitting affects supervised learning models more. A poorly chosen 'k' (number of clusters) can, however, result in results that do not meaningfully represent the data structure. Underfitting is also not a common concern for K-Means. However, if the chosen 'k' is too low, it may oversimplify the data structure, missing important distinctions between data points.

For our model, we must consider whether the number of clusters (k) chosen accurately represents the inherent structure of the data. Metrics such as the silhouette score and the elbow method can help us determine if our model is properly fitting the data. It is critical to strike a balance in which the model is neither too complex nor too simple for the data at hand, ensuring that it generalizes well and provides reliable, actionable insights.

Cross-Validation Technique

Understanding Cross-Validation

Cross-validation is a fundamental technique in machine learning for determining a model's effectiveness, particularly in terms of its performance with unseen data. This method is critical for assessing a model's generalizability, which is essential for ensuring its applicability in real-world scenarios. It entails dividing the entire dataset into multiple subsets, followed by a cycle of training and validating the model on different subsets. A process like this is useful for determining how well the model can adapt and perform on data it has never seen before.

Cross-validation's overarching goal is to reduce the risk of overfitting, a common pitfall in machine learning in which a model performs exceptionally well on its training data but poorly on new, unseen data. Cross-validation ensures that the model's performance is not only accurate but also consistent across different data subsets. This method provides a more nuanced and reliable estimate of the model's performance on a separate dataset, which is critical for determining its real-world applicability. Furthermore, cross-validation greatly aids in model selection by allowing the identification of the model that best captures the underlying trends in the data without overfitting.

Types of Cross-Validation

K-Fold Cross-Validation

The dataset is partitioned into 'k' distinct subsets in this widely used form. The model is trained on 'k-1' of these subsets, with the remaining subset serving as validation. This process is repeated 'k' times to ensure that each subset only serves as validation data once. This method is especially useful for providing a comprehensive evaluation of the model's performance across the entire dataset.

Stratified K-Fold Cross-Validation

This variant is similar to the standard K-Fold, but with one important difference. The folds in Stratified K-Fold Cross-Validation are built by preserving the percentage of samples for each class. This method is especially useful for datasets with unequal class distributions because it ensures that each fold is a representative mix of the various classes, providing a more balanced and accurate assessment of the model's performance.

LOOCV (Leave-One-Out Cross-Validation)

LOOCV is an extreme case of K-Fold Cross-Validation, where 'k' is set equal to the total number of data points in the dataset. Each individual data point is used as a single validation set in this method, while the remaining data points form the training set. While computationally demanding, this approach ensures that the model is tested against every single data point, providing a highly detailed and thorough evaluation of its performance.

Practical Application on K-Means Model

While cross-validation is typically used in supervised learning, it's less common in unsupervised techniques like K-Means. However, we can still employ a form of validation to assess the consistency of our clustering results.

One way to validate our K-Means model is by assessing the stability of the clusters. This involves repeatedly running K-Means and checking how consistently data points are assigned to the same clusters. We can visualize the distribution of cluster assignments across multiple iterations to check for consistency.

For our coffee app data, we should perform a stability check on the K-Means clustering:

```
from collections import defaultdict


# Number of iterations for stability check
n_iterations = 10


# Dictionary to store cluster assignments for each iteration
cluster_assignments = defaultdict(list)


# Repeatedly running K-Means and storing cluster assignments
for i in range(n_iterations):
    kmeans = KMeans(n_clusters=3, random_state=i)
    clusters = kmeans.fit_predict(X)
    for idx, cluster in enumerate(clusters):
        cluster_assignments[idx].append(cluster)


# Visualizing the cluster assignments
```

```
plt.figure(figsize=(15, 8))
for i in cluster_assignments:
    plt.plot(cluster_assignments[i], marker='o', label=f'Data Point {i}')

plt.title('Cluster Assignments Across Iterations')
plt.xlabel('Iteration')
plt.ylabel('Assigned Cluster')
plt.legend()
plt.show()
```

Following is the visualization:

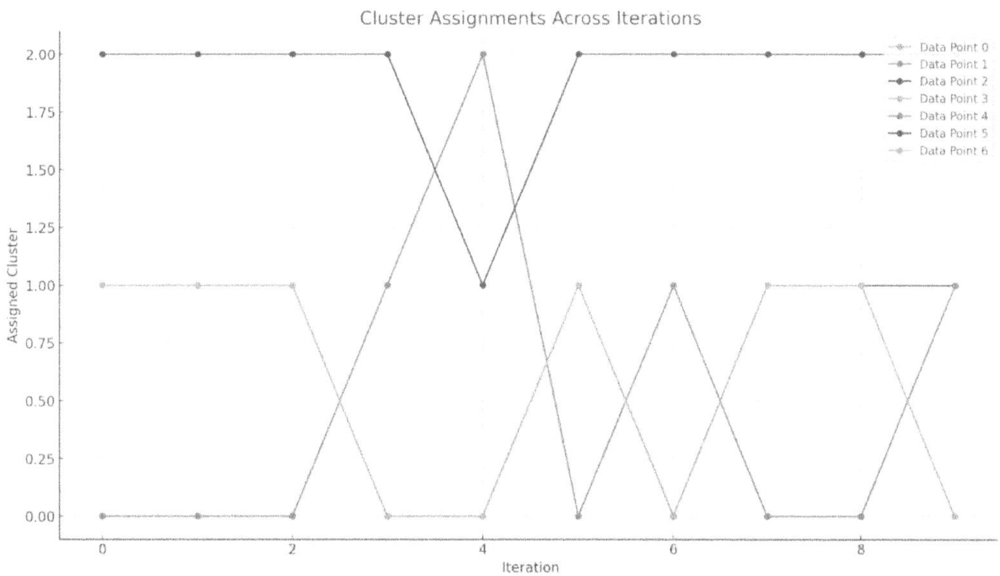

Fig 4.9 Cluster Assignments Across Iterations (Line Plot)

Each line in the above visualization represents a data point, with its cluster assignment shown across different iterations of K-Means. If the lines are relatively flat, it means that a data point is consistently assigned to the same cluster, implying that the clustering process is stable. If the lines, on the other hand, show a lot of variation, this indicates that the clustering is not stable and may not be reliably capturing the true structure of the data.

This type of visualization is useful for assessing the stability of K-Means clusters. Stable cluster assignments across multiple runs can boost confidence in the model's robustness and the identified clusters' dependability.

Hyperparameter Tuning

Overview

Hyperparameter tuning is a significant turning point in machine learning that involves optimizing a model's parameters to improve its performance. Unlike model parameters, which are learned during training, hyperparameters are set before the learning process begins and have a significant impact on the model's behavior and performance.

Hyperparameters are the model's external configurations that cannot be learned from data. They are the parameters that must be specified and tuned in order for a learning algorithm to function optimally. Proper hyperparameter tuning can significantly improve the performance of a model. Finding the sweet spot where the model is neither overfitting nor underfitting is the goal.

Methods of Hyperparameter Tuning

1. Grid Search: Tests every combination of hyperparameters specified in a grid.
2. Random Search: Randomly selects combinations to test, which can be more efficient than grid search.
3. Bayesian Optimization: Uses a probabilistic model to select the most promising hyperparameters to evaluate in the true objective function.

Hyperparameters in K-Means Clustering

For our K-Means model being applied, the main hyperparameter is the number of clusters (k). However, other hyperparameters can also be tuned:

Number of Clusters (k)

This is the most crucial hyperparameter for K-Means. It defines how many clusters the data should be divided into. It can be determined by methods like the Elbow Method, Silhouette Analysis, or Gap Statistic.

Initialization Method

It defines how the initial centroids are chosen. Common methods are 'k-means++' and 'random'. 'k-means++' is generally preferred as it tends to result in better cluster formation.

Number of Initialization Runs (n_init)

This means the number of times the algorithm will be run with different centroid initializations. The final results will be the best output of n_init consecutive runs in terms of inertia. Increasing n_init can improve the chances of escaping local minima but at the cost of computational time.

Maximum Number of Iterations (max_iter)

This means the maximum number of iterations the algorithm runs for a single run. It needs to be high enough to allow convergence but can be capped to control runtime.

Tolerance (tol)

This is defined as a threshold to declare convergence. If centroids change less than this threshold, the algorithm stops. Keeping lower tolerance can lead to more precise results but might increase computation time.

Applying Hyperparameters

We shall now apply some hyperparameter tuning to our K-Means model. We will focus on tuning the number of clusters (k), using the Elbow Method as an example:

```
from sklearn.cluster import KMeans
import matplotlib.pyplot as plt


# Calculating inertia for different k values
inertia = []
for i in range(1, 11):  # Testing 1 to 10 clusters
    kmeans = KMeans(n_clusters=i, random_state=42)
    kmeans.fit(X)
    inertia.append(kmeans.inertia_)


# Plotting the Elbow Method graph
plt.figure(figsize=(10, 6))
plt.plot(range(1, 11), inertia, marker='o')
plt.title('Elbow Method')
plt.xlabel('Number of Clusters')
plt.ylabel('Inertia')
plt.show()
```

Following is the visualization using the Elbow Method for our K-Means clustering model:

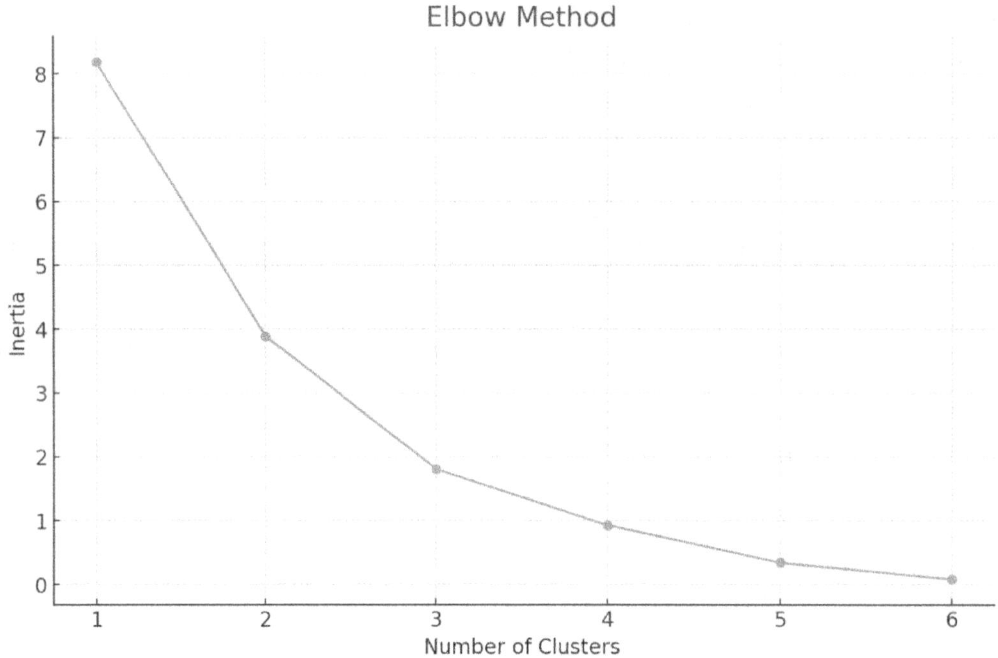

Fig 4.10 Number of Clusters using Elbow Method

In the above graph, the plot shows the inertia for different numbers of clusters (k), ranging from 1 to 6. Inertia refers to the within-cluster sum of squares, which measures the compactness of the clusters. You'll notice that as the number of clusters increases, the inertia decreases. The 'elbow' point in the graph is where the rate of decrease sharply changes. This point indicates the optimal number of clusters for our model. It represents a balance where adding more clusters doesn't provide much better modeling of the data.

In the visualization, you'd look for an 'elbow' where the inertia starts decreasing at a slower rate. This point is a good indicator of the optimal number of clusters. Hyperparameter tuning, particularly in unsupervised learning models like K-Means, is more of an art than an exact science. It requires a combination of domain knowledge, intuition, and experimentation. By tuning the hyperparameters effectively, you can significantly enhance the model's ability to capture the true essence of the data, leading to more meaningful and actionable insights in applications like our coffee preference prediction app. The elbow seems to be around 3 or 4 clusters. This suggests that dividing the coffee preference data into 3 or 4 clusters would be appropriate to capture the significant patterns without overcomplicating the model.

Summary

In this chapter, we learned all about training ML models, with an emphasis on using the K-Means clustering algorithm with the data from our coffee app. The essence of training a model is its ability to learn from data, recognize patterns, and make accurate predictions or categorizations. This training process with K-Means entails determining the optimal number of clusters that best represent the inherent grouping in the data. We learned about how the algorithm iteratively updates cluster centroids to minimize variance within each cluster, enhancing the model's ability to segment data meaningfully.

The tuning of hyperparameters emerged as a critical aspect of refining the K-Means model. We investigated how tuning the number of clusters (k) is critical for the model's effectiveness, using methods such as the Elbow Method to determine the optimal k value. This process aids in striking a balance between over-segmenting the data (which can result in overfitting) and under-segmenting it (which can result in underfitting). The Elbow Method visualization provided a practical approach to understanding and applying this tuning, demonstrating how inertia, or the within-cluster sum of squares, decreases as the number of clusters increases, and how the 'elbow' point serves as an indicator for the optimal number of clusters.

The concept of cross-validation, which is more commonly used in supervised learning, was adapted to assess the stability of our K-Means model. We assessed the consistency of the model's clustering by visualizing the cluster assignments across multiple iterations. While unconventional for unsupervised learning models, this approach provided insights into the clustering process's reliability, ensuring that the patterns identified by the model are robust and not artifacts of specific data sampling or initialization.

The journey through K-Means clustering training, hyperparameter tuning, and validation illuminated the nuances of machine learning model development. It emphasized the significance of not only developing a model but also refining and validating it to ensure its effectiveness and reliability. In the broader context of AI, such meticulous model development and fine-tuning are critical to developing AI applications that are not only intelligent and insightful, but also dependable and accurate in their predictions and analyses. The application of these concepts to the data from our coffee app provided a practical lens through which to view these processes, highlighting how they can be used to extract meaningful insights from real-world data.

CHAPTER 5: ESSENTIALS OF DEEP LEARNING

Overview

We began by learning how algorithms learn from data to make predictions or decisions. We investigated supervised learning, in which models such as decision trees learn from labeled data, and unsupervised learning, in which models such as K-Means search for patterns in data without explicit guidance. Remember how we looked into training models to ensure they weren't simply memorizing data (overfitting) or remaining too simple (underfitting)? And the art of hyperparameter tuning, in which we fine-tuned our models to maximize their performance. These ideas are the foundation of artificial intelligence, allowing machines to learn, adapt, and make intelligent decisions.

We will now dive headfirst into deep learning. Consider deep learning to be a branch of machine learning with a much deeper (literally) level of capability. It's like diving into deeper waters with more diverse and complex sea life.

Deep learning is a subset of machine learning that employs neural networks with multiple layers (hence the name 'deep'). These networks are capable of learning from large amounts of data and identifying patterns that are too complex for humans or traditional machine learning algorithms to identify. Deep learning is powered by neural networks, which are inspired by the structure and function of the human brain. These networks are made up of layers of interconnected nodes (neurons), with each layer transforming the input data so that the next layer can refine it further. Deep learning excels at dealing with large amounts of unstructured data such as images, sound, and text. It's at the heart of some of the most ground-breaking AI applications, ranging from voice assistants like Siri and Alexa to self-driving cars and even disease diagnosis in the medical field.

Deep learning has significantly increased AI's capabilities:

Handling Complex Data

It can process and learn from complex, high-dimensional data like images and videos, making sense of them in a way that was previously impossible.

Feature Learning

Unlike traditional machine learning, where features need to be handcrafted, deep learning algorithms automatically learn the features needed for a task. This automatic feature extraction is a game-changer, especially in areas like computer vision and natural language processing.

Scalability and Versatility

Deep learning models excel as the amount of data increases, making them well-suited for the big data era. They are versatile, tackling a wide range of tasks from classification and regression to generation and reinforcement learning.

Deep learning models are pushing the boundaries of what machines are capable of learning and accomplishing. These models are beginning to understand human language and are also beginning to recognize objects in images. They are not merely models; rather, they are the engines that are driving a significant portion of the modern revolution in artificial intelligence. They are transforming the way in which machines interact with the world and augmenting human capabilities in ways that have never been seen before.

Neural Networks

What Are Neural Networks?

Neural networks are a series of algorithms that mimic the operations of a human brain to recognize relationships between vast amounts of data. They consist of interconnected units or nodes, called artificial neurons, which process data received.

Think of them as layered architectures:

- Input Layer: This is where the network receives its input data.
- Hidden Layers: These layers perform computations through a system of weighted connections and are where most of the processing happens.
- Output Layer: The final layer that outputs the prediction or decision of the network.

How Do Neural Networks Work?

Data is fed into the input layer. Each neuron in the layer receives a piece of this data. Each connection between neurons has a weight, a numerical value that is adjusted during training. The neuron computes the weighted sum of its inputs and then applies an activation function to this sum. The activation function determines whether the neuron should be activated, influencing the network's output.

The process repeats through each layer. The activated neurons in one layer pass on their data to the next layer, transforming the data step-by-step. Backpropagation is the heart of learning in neural networks. When a network makes an error in its output, the error is propagated back through the network. Weights are adjusted to decrease the error, making the model learn from its mistakes.

Types of Neural Networks

1. Feedforward Neural Networks: The simplest type of neural network. Here, the data moves in only one direction – forward – from the input nodes, through the hidden nodes, and to the output nodes.

2. Convolutional Neural Networks (CNNs): Tailored for processing data with a grid-like

topology, such as images. CNNs use a specialized kind of layer called a convolutional layer that can detect patterns like edges, textures, and complex objects in the images.

3. Recurrent Neural Networks (RNNs): Designed for sequential data like time series or natural language. Unlike feedforward networks, RNNs have loops in them, allowing information to persist.

4. Long Short-Term Memory Networks (LSTMs): A special kind of RNN that can learn long-term dependencies. They are crucial in complex sequential tasks like language translation.

5. Autoencoders: Used for unsupervised learning tasks, such as dimensionality reduction or feature learning. They work by compressing the input into a lower-dimensional code and then reconstructing the output from this representation.

6. Generative Adversarial Networks (GANs): Comprise two neural networks, a generator and a discriminator, which compete against each other. GANs are powerful in generating new data that is similar to the training data, like creating realistic images or videos.

Building Neurons and Layers

Transitioning from a K-Means clustering model to a neural network approach involves reimagining how we process our data. We will break down these concepts and then practically demonstrate how to code neurons and layers for a neural network model tailored to our coffee app dataset.

Understanding Layers and Neurons in Neural Networks

Neurons, or nodes, are the basic units of a neural network. Each neuron receives input, processes it, and passes on its output to the next layer. The process within a neuron typically involves summing the input, applying weights, and then passing it through an activation function (though we will not delve into activation functions here).

- Input Layer: The first layer that receives the input data. Each neuron in this layer represents a feature of the input dataset.

- Hidden Layers: Layers between the input and output layers. They are where the complex processing of inputs happens via neurons.

- Output Layer: The final layer that produces the output of the model. The number of neurons in this layer depends on the problem being solved (e.g., one neuron for binary classification).

Sample Program: Building Neural Network

For our coffee preference prediction app, we will conceptualize a simple neural network. Our aim is to predict customer preferences or behaviors based on their previous interactions.

Suppose we want to predict customer satisfaction based on their purchase history and ratings. Our input features could be coffee types and ratings, and the output could be the predicted satisfaction level. We will use the same preprocessed dataset as before, normalized and ready for input into a neural network. And, we will use Python and a library like Keras, which provides a high-level way to build neural networks.

```
import keras
from keras.models import Sequential
from keras.layers import Dense


# Assuming 'X' is our input features and 'y' is the target variable


# Creating a Sequential Model
model = Sequential()


# Adding the Input Layer (assuming 4 features: Espresso, Latte, Cappuccino, Feedback)
model.add(Dense(units=5, input_dim=4))  # 'units' are the number of neurons in the
layer


# Adding a Hidden Layer
model.add(Dense(units=3))  # Adding another layer with 3 neurons


# Adding the Output Layer
# For simplicity, we say we have a binary classification problem (satisfied/unsatisfied)
model.add(Dense(units=1))  # 1 neuron for binary output


# Model summary to visualize the architecture
```

```
model.summary()
```

In the above code snippet,

- Sequential Model: This is a linear stack of layers in Keras, where you can simply add layers
- Dense Layers: These are fully connected layers. 'Dense' implies that each neuron in the layer receives input from all neurons of the previous layer.
- Units: The number of neurons in a layer. The first layer has 5 neurons, the hidden layer has 3, and the output layer has 1 neuron.
- Input Dim: Specifies the number of features in the input data (4 in our case).

You can build the foundation of our coffee app's neural network by executing this code. Although simple, this network serves as the foundation for more complex architectures. It's important to remember that the true power of neural networks lies in their ability to learn intricate patterns from data, which becomes more pronounced with more sophisticated architectures and the incorporation of features such as activation functions, loss functions, and optimizers, which we will look at later.

Neural Network Components

Activation Functions

Activation functions are mathematical equations that determine the output of a neural network. They introduce non-linearity into the network, allowing it to learn and perform more complex tasks.

Following are the functions:

- ReLU (Rectified Linear Unit): Popular for hidden layers. It outputs the input directly if positive, else it outputs zero.
- Sigmoid: Converts values into a range between 0 and 1. Useful for binary classification.
- Softmax: Used in the output layer for multi-class classification. It converts output scores into probability distribution.

Loss Functions

Loss functions, also known as cost functions, are essential in the fields of machine learning and deep learning. They are a critical measure of a model's effectiveness and accuracy, quantitatively expressing how well the model's predictions match the actual data. The essence of these functions is their ability to calculate and quantify the 'loss' between the model's predicted outputs and the true values. This measurement is critical in guiding the model's training process, with the overarching goal of minimizing this loss to improve the model's predictive accuracy.

The choice of an appropriate loss function is a critical decision in model development and is heavily influenced by the nature of the problem being addressed. Because of their distinct characteristics and requirements, different types of problems, such as regression, binary classification, or multi-class classification, necessitate different loss functions.

Binary Cross-Entropy

The Binary Cross-Entropy loss function is commonly used for binary classification tasks, where the outcomes are typically classified into two distinct classes. This function is specifically designed to evaluate the performance of models on tasks where the objective is to differentiate between two possible outcomes, such as 'yes' or 'no', 'true' or 'false'. The binary cross-entropy loss function effectively captures probability error in binary classification models and is useful in refining such models.

Categorical Cross-Entropy

In contrast, the Categorical Cross-Entropy loss function is better suited for tasks involving multi-class classification, where the goal is to categorize data into more than two classes. This function excels at scenarios in which each instance must be classified into one of several classes. It assesses the model's ability to accurately predict the probability for each class and is an important component in training models to effectively classify instances into multiple categories.

Furthermore, for regression problems with continuous output, loss functions such as Mean Squared Error (MSE) or Mean Absolute Error (MAE) are used. These functions compute the difference between predicted and actual numerical values, which is useful in tasks where the goal is to predict a continuous quantity, such as temperature or price.

Optimizers

Optimizers are important in the training process of machine learning, particularly neural networks. They are sophisticated algorithms designed to update and adjust the network's various parameters, such as weights and learning rate, in order to minimize the loss function. Optimizers improve the model's ability to make accurate predictions by refining these parameters. The optimizer used can have a significant impact on the speed and quality of the learning process, and several types have been developed, each with their own set of characteristics and application.:

Gradient Descent

Often regarded as the most fundamental optimizer, Gradient Descent serves as the foundation for more complex optimizers. It uses the entire dataset to perform a single parameter update per iteration. Calculating the gradient of the loss function with respect to the model's parameters and then adjusting those parameters in the opposite direction of the gradient are both steps in the process. By doing so, the optimizer moves closer to the loss function's minimum, where the model's predictions are most accurate. However, because it relies on the entire dataset for each update, it can be computationally demanding, especially for large datasets.

Stochastic Gradient Descent (SGD)

This iteration on the basic Gradient Descent improves efficiency by updating the model's parameters using only a single data point or a small batch of data at a time. Because the updates are stochastic, they introduce randomness, which can aid in escaping local minima and potentially finding a better global minimum. While SGD may be faster and use less memory than standard Gradient Descent, it may also cause more fluctuation in the path to the minimum.

Adam

The Adam optimizer is a more sophisticated approach that combines the benefits of two other optimization algorithms: AdaGrad and RMSProp. Adam is an abbreviation for 'Adaptive Moment Estimation,' and it excels at dealing with large datasets and high-dimensional parameter spaces. It keeps separate learning rates for each parameter and computes adaptive learning rates based on the gradient's first and second moments. Because Adam is efficient with sparse gradients and noisy problems, it is a popular choice in a variety of machine learning applications.

Other optimizers include RMSProp, which is designed to address AdaGrad's diminishing learning rate issues, and Momentum, which accelerates the optimizer in the relevant direction while dampening oscillations. Each optimizer has its own set of advantages and disadvantages, and is chosen based on the specific requirements and characteristics of the neural network and the problem at hand.

Coding Activation Functions, Loss Function, and Optimizer

We shall now add all the above components to our existing neural network model:

```
import keras
from keras.models import Sequential
from keras.layers import Dense

# Assuming 'X' is our input features and 'y' is the target variable
```

```
# Creating the Sequential Model
model = Sequential()

# Adding Layers with Activation Functions
model.add(Dense(units=5, input_dim=4, activation='relu'))  # Input Layer with ReLU
model.add(Dense(units=3, activation='relu'))  # Hidden Layer with ReLU

# Output Layer with Sigmoid (assuming binary classification)
model.add(Dense(units=1, activation='sigmoid'))

# Compiling the Model with Loss Function and Optimizer
model.compile(optimizer='adam', loss='binary_crossentropy', metrics=['accuracy'])

# Model summary
model.summary()
```

In the above code snippet,

- ReLU is used in the hidden layers for non-linear transformation.
- The sigmoid function in the output layer is suitable for binary classification.
- The compile method configures the model with an optimizer, loss function, and additional metrics (like accuracy).
    a. adam optimizer is an efficient choice for most problems.
    b. binary_crossentropy is used as the loss function for binary classification tasks.
    c. Metrics: Accuracy is a common metric for classification tasks.

By running this code, we create a neural network with specific functionalities for each layer and a mechanism to optimize its performance.

Exploring CNNs

Convolutional Neural Networks (CNNs) are a specialized kind of neural network used primarily for processing data with a grid-like topology, such as images. They are exceptional in their ability to detect patterns, such as edges and textures in images, making them ideal for computer vision tasks.

Understanding Convolutional Neural Networks (CNNs)

CNNs are designed to automatically and adaptively learn spatial hierarchies of features from input images. They are adept at reducing the complexities of the image data, making the process efficient and manageable.

Key Components of CNN Architecture

- Convolutional Layer: The core building block of a CNN. It applies a number of filters to the input to create a feature map that highlights features like edges or shapes.
- ReLU Layer: Introduces non-linearity in the model, allowing it to learn more complex patterns.
- Pooling Layer: Reduces the spatial size of the representation, decreasing the number of parameters and computation in the network.
- Fully Connected Layer: After several convolutional and pooling layers, the high-level reasoning in the neural network is done via fully connected layers.

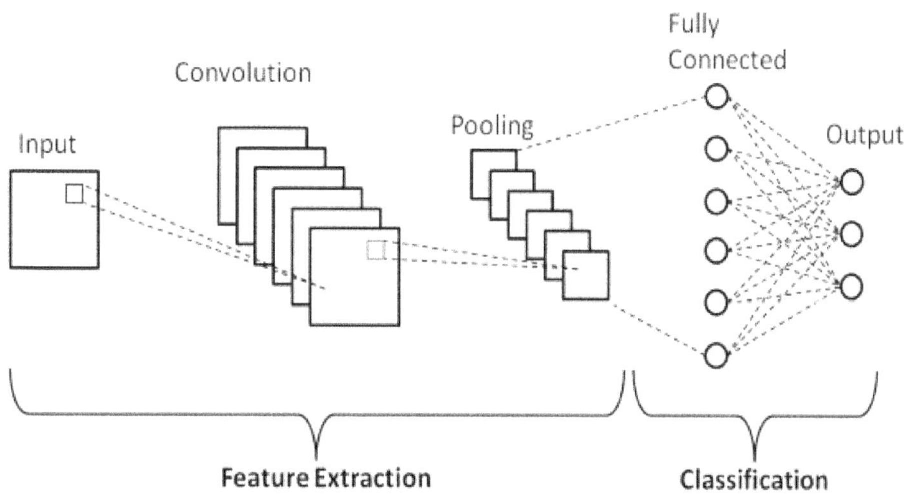

Fig 5.1 CNN Architecture

Designing a CNN

Consider that we want to design a simple CNN to classify images into different categories (like distinguishing between various types of coffee cups). We will use Python and Keras to build this model.

```
from keras.models import Sequential
from keras.layers import Conv2D, MaxPooling2D, Flatten, Dense

# Initialize the CNN
model = Sequential()

# Step 1 - Convolution
model.add(Conv2D(32, (3, 3), input_shape=(64, 64, 3), activation='relu'))

# Step 2 - Pooling
model.add(MaxPooling2D(pool_size=(2, 2)))

# Adding a second convolutional layer (optional)
model.add(Conv2D(32, (3, 3), activation='relu'))
model.add(MaxPooling2D(pool_size=(2, 2)))

# Step 3 - Flattening
model.add(Flatten())

# Step 4 - Full Connection
model.add(Dense(units=128, activation='relu'))
model.add(Dense(units=1, activation='sigmoid')) # Change the units and activation for multi-class classification

# Compile the CNN
model.compile(optimizer='adam', loss='binary_crossentropy', metrics=['accuracy'])
```

```
# Model summary
model.summary()
```

In the above code snippet,

- Conv2D Layer: This is the convolutional layer. We're using 32 filters (kernels), each of size 3x3. The input_shape is (64, 64, 3), which corresponds to 64x64 pixel images with 3 channels (RGB).

- MaxPooling2D Layer: This pooling layer reduces the spatial volume of the input image after convolution.

- Flatten Layer: Converts the 2D matrix data to a vector. This allows it to be fed into the fully connected layer.

- Dense Layer: These are fully connected layers. relu is used for the hidden layer and sigmoid for the output layer. For multi-class classification, use softmax activation and adjust the number of units to match the number of classes.

The above model can be trained on labeled image data and then used to classify new images. The architecture can also be modified and expanded based on the complexity of the task and the specifics of the dataset.

Explore RNNs

Recurrent Neural Networks (RNNs) are a unique class of neural networks particularly suited for sequential data, such as time series, speech, text, or any data where the sequence of elements is crucial. They have internal memory that captures information about previous steps, making them ideal for tasks where context and order matter.

Understanding Recurrent Neural Networks (RNNs)

RNNs process sequences by iterating through the elements and maintaining a 'state' that contains information relative to what it has seen so far. This state acts as a kind of memory that captures information about previous elements in the sequence.

Key Components of RNN Architecture

- Input Layer: Receives the sequence data.
- Recurrent Layer: Processes each element of the sequence one at a time while maintaining an internal state.

- Output Layer: Generates the output, which could be a prediction or a transformed sequence.

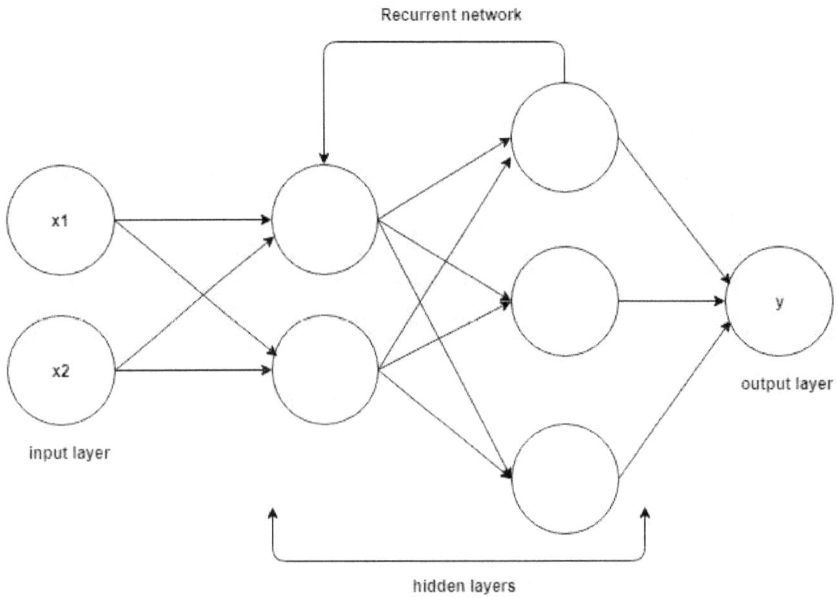

Fig 5.2 RNN Architecture

While RNNs are powerful, they can suffer from issues like vanishing and exploding gradients, making them ineffective at learning long-range dependencies in a sequence. To overcome this, more advanced forms of RNNs, like Long Short-Term Memory (LSTM) networks and Gated Recurrent Units (GRUs), are used.

Designing an RNN

We will design a simple RNN using keras for a sequential task, like predicting the next word in a sentence.

```
from keras.models import Sequential
from keras.layers import SimpleRNN, Dense

# Assuming 'X' is our input sequence and 'y' is the target sequence

# Initialize the RNN
model = Sequential()
```

```
# Adding the RNN layer
# Consider that our input sequences are encoded with 100-dimensional embeddings
model.add(SimpleRNN(units=50, activation='relu', input_shape=(None, 100)))

# Adding the output layer
model.add(Dense(units=1, activation='sigmoid'))  # Modify units and activation based
on your specific task

# Compile the RNN
model.compile(optimizer='adam', loss='binary_crossentropy', metrics=['accuracy'])

# Model summary
model.summary()
```

In the above RNN designing code,

- SimpleRNN Layer: This is the recurrent layer of the network. units=50 means this layer has 50 neurons. input_shape=(None, 100) means the model can take any number of 100-dimensional input vectors.

- Dense Layer: This is the output layer of the network. The number of units and the activation function depends on the specific task (e.g., binary classification, multi-class classification).

- Compile: The model is compiled with an optimizer and a loss function. The choice depends on the task.

This simple RNN model demonstrates how to implement recurrent neural networks in Keras. Because of their ability to capture long-range dependencies more effectively, LSTM or GRU layers should be used instead of the basic SimpleRNN layer for more complex tasks, particularly those involving long sequences.

Train Neural Nets (NNs)

The process of training neural networks or deep learning models is highly important because it teaches the models how to make accurate predictions or decisions based on the data that is provided to them. In order to complete this training, you will need to provide the network with data, give it the opportunity to make predictions, and then modify it based on the accuracy of these predictions. Alternatively, you can simply understand the steps that are followed as below:

Forward Propagation

- In this stage, input data is fed into the neural network.
- The network processes this data layer by layer, from the input layer through any hidden layers, and finally to the output layer.
- Each neuron in the network applies a weighted sum of its inputs and a bias, followed by an activation function to produce its output.
- The final output is the network's prediction based on its current weights.

Calculating the Loss

- After forward propagation, the network's predictions are compared with the actual target values (the ground truth).
- A loss function quantifies the difference between the predictions and the actual values. Common loss functions include Mean Squared Error for regression tasks and Cross-Entropy for classification tasks.
- The loss provides a measure of how 'off' the network's predictions are from the actual values.

Backpropagation

- Backpropagation is the process of tracing the loss back through the network to understand how each weight contributed to the error.
- By applying the chain rule of calculus, the partial derivatives of the loss with respect to each weight (i.e., the gradients) are calculated.
- These gradients indicate how much a change in each weight would affect the loss, providing a roadmap for adjusting the weights to reduce the loss.

Weight Update

- The weights of the network are adjusted to minimize the loss. This adjustment is supervised by the gradients calculated during backpropagation.
- Optimization algorithms, such as Gradient Descent or Adam, are used to update the weights. These algorithms determine the extent and direction of the weight adjustments.
- The learning rate, a hyperparameter, controls how big a step is taken in the direction indicated by the gradients during each update.

Iteration (Epochs)

- The entire process of forward propagation, loss calculation, backpropagation, and weight update is repeated over multiple iterations, known as epochs.
- In each epoch, the network processes the entire training dataset, learning and adjusting its weights to minimize the loss.
- With each epoch, the network's predictions should ideally become more accurate, and the loss should decrease.

Training Deep Learning Model

Training deep learning models, such as a Convolutional Neural Network (CNN) for image classification and a Recurrent Neural Network (RNN) for sequential data, involves a series of steps that prepare the model to make accurate predictions. We will simplify and explain these steps using our previous examples: the CNN for classifying coffee cup images and the RNN for word prediction.

Coffee Cup Image Classification using CNN

Preparing the Data

The images of coffee cups and their corresponding labels (like 'empty', 'full', 'half-full') are gathered. Each image is processed to ensure consistency. This includes resizing the images to a uniform size and normalizing the pixel values (so they are in a similar range, typically between 0 and 1).

Model Compilation

The CNN model, as we created in our example, needs to be configured for training. This involves choosing a loss function (like 'categorical_crossentropy' for multi-class classification) and an optimizer (like 'adam' which helps in adjusting the weights effectively). This step sets the ground rules on how the model will learn from the data.

Fitting the Model

Here, the model learns from the data. Using the fit method in Keras, we provide the model with our images (inputs) and labels (desired outputs).

Sample Command::

```
model.fit(images, labels, epochs=10, batch_size=32).
```

The model goes through the images and labels, learning to associate specific image features with their corresponding labels, over 10 cycles (epochs).

Training Word Prediction using RNN

For word prediction, we start with a large text (like a book or a collection of sentences). The text is converted into sequences of words or characters. These sequences are then transformed into a format that the RNN can understand (like numerical encodings).

Similar to the CNN, the RNN is prepared for training by selecting a loss function and an optimizer. For word prediction, 'binary_crossentropy' is a common choice for the loss function, and 'adam' is a popular optimizer. This configures how the RNN will learn to predict the next word in a sequence.

The RNN is trained using the fit method. Here, the input is a sequence of words, and the output is the next word that follows the sequence.

Sample Command:

```
model.fit(sequence_data, next_words, epochs=20, batch_size=64).
```

The RNN then learns to predict the next word in a sequence based on the patterns it observes in the training data, over 20 cycles (epochs).

In both cases, the models learn by adjusting their internal weights to reduce the difference between their predictions and the actual data. This process is repeated over multiple epochs, improving the model's accuracy with each pass through the data.

Fine-tuning Models

Fine-tuning neural networks helps in achieving optimal performance from your models. It involves adjusting various hyperparameters, which are the knobs and dials of your model, to improve its learning and prediction capabilities. We will explore some key hyperparameters, including the number of hidden layers and neurons, learning rate, and batch size, and learn how to fine-tune them.

Number of Hidden Layers

Hidden layers are crucial for a neural network as they add depth, allowing the model to learn complex features. However, the number of these layers needs careful consideration. With too few layers, the network might fail to capture complex patterns, leading to underfitting. Conversely, too many layers can cause overfitting and increase computational demands. A good starting point is to use one or two hidden layers for simpler tasks, gradually increasing this number for more complex problems while monitoring the impact on performance.

Number of Neurons per Hidden Layer

The neurons within each layer are responsible for capturing different features from the input data. The number of neurons is another aspect that requires fine-tuning. Having too few neurons might result in underfitting as the network may not capture enough complexity. On the other hand, too many neurons can lead to higher computational costs and a greater risk of overfitting. A common approach is to create a funnel-like structure, where the number of neurons decreases in subsequent layers, though this isn't a strict rule.

Learning Rate

The learning rate is a key parameter that determines the size of the steps the network takes during the optimization process. If the learning rate is too high, the network might overshoot the minimum loss, while a too low learning rate can slow down the learning process and cause the network to get stuck in local minima. Using adaptive learning rates, such as learning rate schedules or optimizers like Adam, can be an effective strategy to address this issue.

Batch Size

Batch size refers to the number of training samples used in one iteration of model training. A larger batch size can speed up the training process but might negatively affect the model's ability to generalize. Conversely, a smaller batch size, while potentially leading to better generalization due to more frequent updates, can slow down the training. Finding the right balance is crucial, and experimenting with different sizes is advisable. Batch sizes that are powers of 2, such as 32, 64, or 128, are commonly used due to computational efficiency.

Sample Program: Fine Tuning CNN Model

We will apply this to fine-tuning the CNN model from our earlier example:

```
from keras.models import Sequential
from keras.layers import Conv2D, MaxPooling2D, Flatten, Dense, Dropout


model = Sequential()
model.add(Conv2D(32, (3, 3), input_shape=(64, 64, 3), activation='relu'))
model.add(MaxPooling2D(pool_size=(2, 2)))
model.add(Conv2D(64, (3, 3), activation='relu'))  # Increased filters
model.add(MaxPooling2D(pool_size=(2, 2)))
model.add(Flatten())
```

```
model.add(Dense(units=128, activation='relu'))
model.add(Dropout(0.5)) # Adding Dropout
model.add(Dense(units=1, activation='sigmoid'))
model.compile(optimizer='adam', loss='binary_crossentropy', metrics=['accuracy'])
```

In the above code snippet,

- Increased Filters: More filters in the second convolutional layer to capture more complex features.
- Dropout: Added to reduce overfitting by randomly dropping units.
- Optimizer: Adam is used for its adaptive learning rate capabilities.

Fine-tuning is often an iterative and experimental process, requiring a balance between model complexity and generalization capability. It's crucial to monitor the model's performance on both training and validation data to ensure it's learning effectively and not just memorizing the training data.

Summary

In this chapter, we explored the advanced world of artificial intelligence, connecting machine learning to deep learning. This investigation was centered on neural networks, specifically their specialized forms: Convolutional Neural Networks (CNNs) for dealing with grid-like data like images, and Recurrent Neural Networks (RNNs) for dealing with sequential data like text or time series. With their distinct architectures and processing capabilities, these networks opened up a plethora of possibilities, ranging from image classification to language processing, demonstrating the versatility and depth of deep learning.

In practice, we walked through the development of a CNN to classify images, which involved establishing layers to detect patterns and reduce complexity, as well as an RNN designed for sequence prediction, emphasizing the importance of sequential data processing. These examples demonstrated not only the coding aspects, but also how these networks learn and process information. CNNs' sequential and hierarchical learning, as well as RNNs' memory-preserving attributes, were key highlights, demonstrating how deep learning models capture and use data characteristics in ways that traditional machine learning models cannot.

Training neural networks emerged as a critical phase, involving not only data transmission through the network but also the complex process of backpropagation and optimization. The concepts of forward propagation, loss calculation, and weight adjustment via backpropagation were dissected, emphasizing how important these processes are to a model's ability to learn from data. Our CNN and RNN model training served as practical examples, demonstrating the path from raw data to a trained model capable of making predictions or processing data sequences.

Finally, the chapter delves into the complexities of fine-tuning neural networks. Adjusting key hyperparameters such as the number of hidden layers and neurons, learning rate, and batch size was required. Fine-tuning is a balancing act in which the goal is to improve the model's ability to learn effectively while avoiding overfitting or underfitting. Our section on fine-tuning provided a framework for approaching this task, demonstrating its importance in the development of effective and efficient deep learning models. This process, which is essential for achieving optimal performance, was demonstrated by modifying our CNN model by incorporating elements such as dropout and experimenting with different numbers of filters and neurons.

CHAPTER 6: NLP AND COMPUTER VISION

Natural Language Processing Overview

Imagine a world in which computers are perfectly capable of comprehending, interpreting, and responding to human language in the same natural way that we do. That encapsulates the nucleus of NLP. It is a field that aims to enable machines to understand and process human language, and it is located at the intersection of computer science, artificial intelligence, and linguistics.

In recent years, natural language processing (NLP) technology has made incredible strides, which has had a significant impact on how we interact with technology. The use of natural language processing (NLP) is becoming increasingly integrated into our digital experiences, beginning with voice assistants such as Siri and Alexa and progressing to customer service chatbots and translation services such as Google Translate. Natural language processing (NLP) systems have become more sophisticated as a result of advancements in machine learning and deep learning. These systems are now able to comprehend context, sentiment, and even subtleties in human language.

Natural language processing (NLP) encompasses a wide variety of tasks, each of which presents its own set of challenges and applications:

- In the context of email spam detection, text classification refers to the process of classifying text into predetermined categories.
- The process of determining which opinions or feelings are contained within a text, such as determining the feelings of customers based on reviews.
- The process of translating text from one language to another using a machine, with the goal of achieving both accuracy and fluency in the translation.
- The process of extracting specific entities (such as names, places, and organizations) from text is referred to as Named Entity Recognition (NER).
- The process of identifying part of speech in a sentence, such as nouns, verbs, and adjectives, is referred to as speech tagging.
- Speech recognition refers to the process of extracting text from spoken language.
- Generation of language refers to the process of producing text that is coherent and contextually relevant based on input.
- Structures that are able to respond to questions posed in natural language are referred to as question answering systems.

In earlier methods, tasks such as text classification or spam detection were accomplished by combining feature engineering with machine learning algorithms such as Naive Bayes, Decision Trees, or Support Vector Machines. The methods in question frequently had difficulty comprehending the context, and they necessitated a substantial amount of data preprocessing.

With the advent of deep learning, natural language processing (NLP) has been revolutionized, and models are now able to learn from vast amounts of text data without the need for explicit feature engineering. Especially in tasks such as language translation and sentiment analysis, models such as recurrent neural networks (RNNs), long short-term memory (LSTMs), and transformers have been game-changers. New benchmarks have been established in the field of natural language processing (NLP) by models such as BERT (Bidirectional Encoder Representations from Transformers), which provide remarkable context-awareness in language comprehension.

NLP has been an essential component in the development of chatbots and virtual assistants. These systems make use of natural language processing (NLP) to comprehend user inquiries and respond in a manner that is human-like. There is a wide range of applications for chatbots, ranging from customer service bots to therapeutic bots like Woebot.

Newly developed models in the field of natural language processing (NLP) include the Generative Pre-trained Transformer 3 (GPT-3). As a result of their training on massive datasets, they are able to generate text that is both remarkably coherent and contextually relevant. This demonstrates the potential of natural language processing (NLP) in a variety of fields, as LLMs are able to write creative fiction, generate code, automate content creation, and more.

The field of natural language processing (NLP) is a demonstration of how far artificial intelligence has progressed in terms of comprehending and interacting with human language. The role that natural language processing (NLP) plays in the contemporary digital landscape is both foundational and transformative. Its applications range from automating mundane tasks to opening up new avenues in human-computer interaction. By bridging the gap between human linguistic capabilities and machine understanding, its future, which is intertwined with advancements in machine learning and deep learning, promises to integrate language processing in our everyday lives in a manner that is even more sophisticated and seamless.

NLP Dataset

For this chapter, we will create a dataset that can be used for a variety of NLP tasks, such as text classification, sentiment analysis, named entity recognition, and more. We will begin by defining the scope and characteristics of our dataset before moving on to the practical side of creating it.

Defining the NLP Dataset

To align with the context of our coffee app, we will create a dataset of customer reviews of various coffee products. Product ratings, textual feedback, timestamps, and customer demographics can all be included in this dataset.

Data Features

1. Review Text: The main body of the review, which includes customer opinions and experiences.
2. Rating: Numerical rating given by the customer, say on a scale of 1 to 5.

3. Timestamp: The date and time when the review was posted.
4. Product ID: A unique identifier for the coffee product being reviewed.
5. Customer Information: This can include anonymized customer IDs and demographic data like age group or location (optional, for more advanced analysis).

Generating Dataset

We will create a simple Python script to generate this dataset. We will use libraries like pandas for data manipulation and Faker for generating realistic-looking textual data.

First, install Faker if you don't have it:

```
pip install faker
```

We then write the script to generate the dataset:

```
import pandas as pd
from faker import Faker
import random

faker = Faker()

# Number of samples to generate
num_samples = 1000

# Generating the dataset
data = {
    'Product_ID': [random.randint(100, 110) for _ in range(num_samples)],
    'Timestamp': [faker.date_time_this_year() for _ in range(num_samples)],
    'Rating': [random.randint(1, 5) for _ in range(num_samples)],
    'Review_Text': [faker.text(max_nb_chars=200) for _ in range(num_samples)]
}
```

```
df = pd.DataFrame(data)

# Display the first few rows of our dataset
print(df.head())
```

As per the above script, following is the sample of the simulated NLP dataset generated:

Customer_ID	Timestamp	Favorite_Coffee	Rating	Review_Text
1039	2023-04-06 04:43:04	Mocha	2	Hit task affect manage page able
1067	2023-08-02 20:35:21	Espresso	1	Represent step cell majority visit only
1047	2023-09-16 03:45:46	Espresso	1	Similar military attention chair want something.
1016	2023-05-11 19:43:17	Latte	3	Sometimes whole voice artist else fine
1032	2023-10-08 02:42:23	Cappuccino	2	Forward structure weight produce prevent

The dataset includes:

- Customer_ID: A unique identifier for each customer.
- Timestamp: The date and time when the review or rating was recorded.
- Favorite_Coffee: The type of coffee preferred by the customer (e.g., Espresso, Latte, Cappuccino, etc.).
- Rating: The customer's rating for their favorite coffee, on a scale of 1 to 5.
- Review_Text: A simulated text review, reflecting the customer's thoughts or experiences.

This dataset, designed with a focus on coffee preference, is more aligned with the theme of our book and will serve as a consistent basis for exploring various NLP tasks and operations throughout this chapter. As we progress through this chapter, we will dive into different NLP methodologies, applying them to this dataset to extract meaningful insights and demonstrate practical applications of NLP.

Text Preprocessing

Text preprocessing is a critical step in NLP where raw text data is cleaned and formatted to enhance the efficiency and effectiveness of NLP models. This process involves various techniques to transform the text into a more manageable and uniform format. We will explore key text preprocessing steps and apply them to our coffee preferences dataset.

Tokenization

It is fundamentally breaking down a text into individual words or phrases. In essence, it's about splitting sentences into smaller components called tokens, which can be words or subwords. It's the first step in understanding the structure of the text. Tokenization helps in analyzing and processing each word individually, which is crucial for tasks like sentiment analysis or topic modeling.

Lowercasing

This is all about converting all text to lowercase. This ensures uniformity in the text. For example, 'Coffee', 'COFFEE', and 'coffee' are treated as the same word. It helps in reducing the complexity of text processing, as the model doesn't need to understand variations in casing.

Removing Punctuation and Special Characters

It eliminates characters like commas, periods, exclamation marks, and other non-alphabetic characters. Punctuation and special characters are often not necessary for many NLP tasks. Removing them reduces the complexity of the text and helps the model focus on the words that carry the core meaning.

Removing Stop Words

This involves filtering out common words such as 'and', 'the', 'is', which appear frequently in text but often don't contribute much to its overall meaning. Stop words can skew the analysis of text data because of their high occurrence. Removing them helps in focusing on words that are more relevant to the context or sentiment of the text.

Stemming and Lemmatization

Both are techniques to reduce words to their base or root form. Stemming chops off the ends of words, often leading to incomplete and imprecise meanings. Lemmatization, on the other hand, considers the context and converts the word to its meaningful base form. They help in reducing the inflectional forms of each word to a common base form, thereby reducing the complexity of the text. This is particularly useful in grouping together different forms of the same word, which aids in tasks like text classification or clustering.

Performing Preprocessing on the Dataset

We will begin with putting each of the above described preprocessing steps for simplifying the text data, making it more tractable for NLP models to process and analyze. NLTK is the perfect python library to begin with.

First, ensure we have NLTK installed:

```
pip install nltk
```

We then preprocess the 'Review_Text' column in our dataset:

```
import nltk
from nltk.corpus import stopwords
from nltk.tokenize import word_tokenize
from nltk.stem import WordNetLemmatizer
import string

# Download necessary NLTK resources
nltk.download('punkt')
nltk.download('stopwords')
nltk.download('wordnet')

# Initializing the lemmatizer
lemmatizer = WordNetLemmatizer()

# Function to preprocess text
def preprocess_text(text):
    # Tokenize the text
    tokens = word_tokenize(text)

    # Convert to lower case
```

```
    tokens = [token.lower() for token in tokens]

    # Remove punctuation and non-alphabetic characters
    tokens = [token for token in tokens if token.isalpha()]

    # Remove stopwords
    stop_words = set(stopwords.words('english'))
    tokens = [token for token in tokens if token not in stop_words]

    # Lemmatize
    tokens = [lemmatizer.lemmatize(token) for token in tokens]

    return ' '.join(tokens)

# Apply the preprocessing to the Review_Text column
df['Processed_Review_Text'] = df['Review_Text'].apply(preprocess_text)

# Display the first few rows of the processed dataset
df[['Review_Text', 'Processed_Review_Text']].head()
```

In the above script,

- We tokenize each review, convert it to lowercase, remove punctuation and non-alphabetic characters, filter out stopwords, and then apply lemmatization.
- The preprocess_text function encapsulates all these steps and is applied to each review in the dataset.
- The result is a new column in our DataFrame, Processed_Review_Text, which contains the preprocessed text.

This preprocessing transforms the raw reviews into a cleaner, more analysis-friendly format, laying the groundwork for subsequent NLP tasks like sentiment analysis, topic modeling, or feature extraction for machine learning models.

Tokenization

Tokenization is a fundamental step in natural language processing (NLP), where we break down text into smaller units called tokens. These tokens are typically words, phrases, or other meaningful elements of language. The process of tokenization lays the groundwork for almost all NLP tasks, from simple text classification to complex language understanding and generation.

Understanding Tokenization

It's the process of splitting textual content into smaller, more manageable parts or tokens. In most cases, these tokens are individual words, but they can also be phrases or symbols depending on the level of granularity needed. Tokenization helps in structuring the text data for further analysis. It's the first step in transforming unstructured text into a format that algorithms can understand and work with.

Very oftenly, text comes with complexities like contractions (e.g., "don't" as "do" and "not"), special characters, or varying delimiters (e.g., spaces, commas). Handling these variations correctly is crucial for accurate tokenization.

Process of Tokenization

Choose the Level of Tokenization

Decide whether the tokens should be words, sentences, or subwords. This decision depends on the task at hand.

Handle Special Cases

Identify and handle special cases like contractions, punctuation marks, or special symbols.

Choose a Tokenizer

Implement a custom tokenizer or choose an existing one from libraries like NLTK, spaCy, or TensorFlow.

Tokenizing Dataset

We will apply tokenization to our coffee preferences dataset, specifically focusing on the Review_Text column. We will use NLTK, a popular Python library for NLP tasks, to tokenize the text data.

First, ensure you have NLTK installed and then proceed with the following script:

```
import nltk
from nltk.tokenize import word_tokenize

# Download the NLTK tokenizer models
nltk.download('punkt')

# Function to tokenize text
def tokenize_text(text):
    tokens = word_tokenize(text)
    return tokens

# Applying tokenization to the Review_Text column
df['Tokens'] = df['Review_Text'].apply(tokenize_text)

# Display the first few rows of the dataset with tokens
df[['Review_Text', 'Tokens']].head()
```

In the above script,

- We use word_tokenize from NLTK, which is a pre-built tokenizer for splitting text into words.
- The tokenize_text function takes a string of text and returns a list of tokens.
- We then apply this function to the Review_Text column of our dataset, creating a new column Tokens that contains the tokenized text.

This tokenization process transforms the raw review text into a list of words, providing a structured format that can be used for further NLP tasks like sentiment analysis, keyword extraction, or even feeding into more advanced models like RNNs or Transformers for deeper language understanding.

Vectorization Approach

Vectorization is the process of converting text data into numerical formats that machine learning algorithms can understand and process. The primary methods include one-hot encoding, bag of words (BoW), bag of n-grams, and Term Frequency-Inverse Document Frequency (TF-IDF). Understanding these approaches will equip you with essential tools for transforming textual data into actionable insights.

One-Hot Encoding

In one-hot encoding, each word in the vocabulary is represented as a vector with a length equal to the vocabulary size. Each vector has a '1' in the position corresponding to the word and '0's elsewhere. One-hot encoding is simple but can become impractical with large vocabularies due to high dimensionality and sparsity.

Bag of Words (BoW)

The BoW model represents text as the frequency of words within the document. It disregards the order of words, focusing only on the frequency or presence of words. It represents each document as a vector indicating the frequency of each word in the vocabulary. BoW loses the order of words, which can be important in many contexts. It also treats all words as equally important.

Bag of N-Grams

An extension of BoW, n-grams are contiguous sequences of 'n' items from a given sample of text or speech. For example, bigrams (2-grams) are pairs of adjacent words. N-grams capture some context and word order, making the model more expressive than simple BoW.

Term Frequency-Inverse Document Frequency (TF-IDF)

TF-IDF measures the importance of a word in a document in a collection of documents. It increases proportionally to the number of times a word appears in the document but is offset by the frequency of the word in the corpus. It helps in understanding the importance or relevance of words within documents in a corpus.

Sample Program: Applying BoW and TF-IDF

We will apply BoW and TF-IDF vectorization to our coffee preferences dataset as an example:

```
from sklearn.feature_extraction.text import CountVectorizer, TfidfVectorizer
```

```
# Bag of Words
bow_vectorizer = CountVectorizer()
bow = bow_vectorizer.fit_transform(df['Review_Text'])

# TF-IDF
tfidf_vectorizer = TfidfVectorizer()
tfidf = tfidf_vectorizer.fit_transform(df['Review_Text'])

# Displaying the feature names for BoW
# Displaying first 10 for brevity
print("BoW Feature Names:", bow_vectorizer.get_feature_names_out()[:10])
```

In the above script,

- CountVectorizer creates a BoW model, transforming the text into a sparse matrix of word counts.
- TfidfVectorizer computes the TF-IDF scores for each word in the documents.
- We then display the first ten feature names from the BoW model for a glimpse of the vocabulary.

These vectorization techniques transform our raw textual data into numerical formats, allowing us to apply machine learning algorithms for various NLP tasks like classification, clustering, or sentiment analysis.

Word Embeddings

The concept of word embeddings is a powerful representation that goes beyond simple counts and frequencies. Word embeddings provide a way to represent words in a dense, continuous vector space and capture much more information about words, including semantic meaning and context.

Understanding Word Embeddings

Word embeddings are learned representations of words where each word is mapped to a dense vector in a continuous vector space. Each dimension in this vector represents latent features of the word, often capturing semantic and syntactic properties.

Unlike one-hot encoding or BoW, embeddings capture the context and relationships between words. Words with similar meanings tend to have similar vectors, enabling the model to understand word associations and nuances.

Popular Word Embedding Models

Word2Vec

Developed by Google researchers, Word2Vec is a game-changing word embedding model that uses neural networks to learn word associations from a large corpus of text. Word2Vec's central idea is to represent words in a multidimensional space where the distance and direction between words reflect their semantic and syntactic similarities. Word2Vec can be implemented using either the Continuous Bag-of-Words (CBOW) or the Skip-Gram architecture. CBOW predicts a target word based on its context, whereas Skip-Gram predicts context words from a target word. This model is well-known for its efficiency, simplicity, and the high quality of learned representations, which can capture complex word relationships such as synonyms, antonyms, and analogies.

GloVe (Global Vectors for Word Representation)

GloVe is another influential word embedding model developed by Stanford researchers. Unlike Word2Vec, which is based on word context, GloVe creates an explicit word-word co-occurrence matrix from the entire corpus, capturing global statistics. The word vectors are then generated using matrix factorization techniques. GloVe's main advantage is its ability to use both global statistics and local context, resulting in word embeddings that encapsulate broader contexts across the entire corpus. This model has been widely used in various NLP applications and has been successful in capturing nuanced word relationships.

FastText

FastText is an extension of the Word2Vec model proposed by Facebook's AI Research lab. While Word2Vec and GloVe generate word embeddings using words as the smallest unit, FastText takes it a step further by taking into account sub-word units (n-grams). For example, the word "apple" can be subdivided into "ap", "app", "appl", "apple", "pp", "ppl", "pple", "pl", "ple", and "le". FastText can now generate representations for out-of-vocabulary (OOV) words by aggregating the vectors of its sub-words, which is a significant improvement over previous models, which could only handle words seen during training. FastText is especially useful when dealing with morphologically rich languages or when the corpus is insufficient to cover all relevant words.

Sample Program: Applying Word Embeddings

We will use GloVe embeddings for our practical walkthrough.

First, download a pre-trained GloVe model from the following link:
https://nlp.stanford.edu/data/glove.6B.zip

From the zip file, we will use glove.6B.50d.txt, which contains 50-dimensional vectors for 6 billion words.

```
import numpy as np

# Load GloVe model
def load_glove_model(glove_file):
    with open(glove_file, 'r', encoding='utf8') as f:
        model = {}
        for line in f:
            split_line = line.split()
            word = split_line[0]
            embedding = np.array([float(val) for val in split_line[1:]])
            model[word] = embedding
        return model

glove_model = load_glove_model('glove.6B.50d.txt')

# Function to vectorize text using GloVe
def vectorize_text(text, model):
    words = text.split()
    word_vectors = [model[word] for word in words if word in model]
    return np.mean(word_vectors, axis=0) if word_vectors else np.zeros(50)

# Apply vectorization to the Review_Text column
df['Embeddings'] = df['Review_Text'].apply(lambda x: vectorize_text(x, glove_model))
```

```
# Display the first few rows of the dataset with embeddings
df[['Review_Text', 'Embeddings']].head()
```

From the above script, we learned the following:

- The load_glove_model function loads the pre-trained GloVe model from the file.
- vectorize_text function vectorizes the review text by averaging the embeddings of the words present in the text.
- Each review in the Review_Text column is transformed into a 50-dimensional vector representing its embedding.

Visualize Word Embeddings

To visualize word embeddings, we can use techniques like t-SNE (t-Distributed Stochastic Neighbor Embedding), which reduces the high-dimensional vectors to two or three dimensions suitable for plotting.

Following is the process how you can visualize GloVe embeddings using t-SNE:

Prepare Your Data

Ensure you have a DataFrame with a column of text data and another column containing the corresponding GloVe embeddings. Depending on the size of your dataset, you might want to sample a subset of your data for efficient processing.

Apply t-SNE

Use t-SNE to reduce the dimensions of your embeddings. Typically, you reduce the dimensions to 2 for easy visualization.

Plot the Results

Plot the reduced embeddings using a scatter plot to visualize the clusters and relationships.

```
from sklearn.manifold import TSNE
import matplotlib.pyplot as plt

# Sample a subset for visualization
subset = df.sample(n=100)
```

```
# Apply t-SNE to the embeddings
tsne = TSNE(n_components=2, random_state=0)
reduced_embeddings = tsne.fit_transform(list(subset['Embeddings']))

# Plotting
plt.figure(figsize=(10, 6))
plt.scatter(reduced_embeddings[:, 0], reduced_embeddings[:, 1])
plt.title("t-SNE visualization of GloVe embeddings")
plt.show()
```

Here,

- We use t-SNE to reduce the 50-dimensional embeddings to 2 dimensions.
- Then we plot these reduced embeddings, where each point represents a review.

This visualization will help you understand the structure of your text data in the embedding space, potentially revealing patterns, clusters, or relationships that are not immediately apparent in the high-dimensional space. It's a powerful way to gain insights into the nature of textual data and the efficacy of your embeddings.

Introduction to Computer Vision

Brief Understanding

Computer Vision (CV) is the process of processing and analyzing digital images and videos in order to extract meaningful information, similar to how human vision works. Computer Vision is fundamentally concerned with teaching machines to interpret and comprehend the visual world. Computer vision algorithms can detect, classify, and track objects or actions using digital images from cameras and videos. This process entails not only identifying shapes and objects in an image, but also comprehending these elements in context.

Deep learning, in particular, has accelerated the evolution of computer vision. Convolutional Neural Networks (CNNs) have played an important role in the advancement of CV tasks, allowing for more accurate and reliable image and video analysis.

Applications of Computer Vision

Computer vision has found applications in a diverse range of fields:

Healthcare: Medical imaging analysis, such as MRI and CT scans interpretation, aiding in diagnostics.

Automotive Industry: Autonomous vehicles use CV for object detection and navigation.

Retail: Analyzing customer behavior, managing inventory, and enhancing shopping experiences through facial recognition and surveillance.

Manufacturing: Quality control through inspection of products on assembly lines.

Agriculture: Crop monitoring and predictive analysis for disease detection in plants.

Entertainment: Augmented Reality (AR) and Virtual Reality (VR) applications.

Security and Surveillance: Facial recognition and activity monitoring for safety and security purposes.

Computer Vision Model

A typical computer vision model, especially those using deep learning, often follows this structure:

Image Preprocessing

Input images are preprocessed to bring them to a uniform size and format. This step might include resizing, normalization, and augmentation techniques to diversify the training data.

Feature Extraction

The model extracts features from the image. This is where CNNs excel, as they automatically detect features like edges, textures, and more complex patterns through their layers.

Classification/Recognition Layer

After feature extraction, these features are fed into additional layers (often fully connected layers) to classify or identify objects within the images.

Output

The final layer outputs the interpretation of the image. This could be a classification label, detection of objects within the image, or pixel-wise segmentation.

Training the Model

Models are trained using large datasets of labeled images. The training involves optimizing the model to reduce the difference between its predictions and the actual labels.

Evaluation and Optimization

The model is evaluated using metrics like accuracy, precision, recall, and F1-score. Further optimization may include hyperparameter tuning and training with augmented datasets.

The general structure of a CV model, though may vary based on the specific task, typically involves layers of processing and interpretation, from raw pixel data to actionable insights or decisions.

Image Processing

Overview

Image processing refers to the technique of performing operations on images to enhance them or extract useful information. Unlike computer vision, which focuses on understanding and interpreting images, image processing is primarily about treating the image as a two-dimensional signal and applying standard signal processing techniques to it.

The objectives can vary from improving the visual appearance of images, to preparing them for further analysis (like object detection in computer vision), to compressing for efficient storage and transmission.

Image Processing Procedure

Image processing generally involves the following steps:

Image Acquisition

This is the first step where an image is captured by a sensor (like a camera) or obtained from a source (like loading from a file).

Preprocessing

1. Noise Reduction: Removing noise from images to enhance quality. Techniques like Gaussian blurring or median filtering are often used.
2. Contrast Enhancement: Adjusting the image contrast to make objects in the image more distinguishable.
3. Normalization: Scaling pixel values to a standard range, often necessary for consistent processing.

Image Transformation

1. Transforming images into a more suitable form for analysis. This includes tasks like:

2. Edge Detection: Identifying sharp edges in the image to understand object boundaries.
3. Color Space Conversion: Changing the color representation (e.g., from RGB to grayscale or HSV).

Feature Extraction

Extracting specific attributes or features from the image. This step is crucial for pattern recognition and computer vision tasks.

Image Segmentation

Dividing the image into multiple segments (sets of pixels) to simplify or change its representation. It's widely used in object detection and recognition.

Post-Processing

Enhancing or altering the image after processing. This might include tasks like sharpening, smoothing, or adding filters.

Analysis and Interpretation

The final step involves analyzing the processed image to extract meaningful information or making decisions based on the image data.

Sample Program: Using OpenCV

We will apply basic image processing techniques using Python and OpenCV, a popular library for image processing and computer vision tasks:

First, ensure you have OpenCV installed:

```
pip install opencv-python
```

We then write a script to load an image, convert it to grayscale, and apply a simple edge detection:

```
import cv2
import matplotlib.pyplot as plt

# Load an image
image = cv2.imread('path_to_image.jpg')
```

```
# Convert to grayscale
gray_image = cv2.cvtColor(image, cv2.COLOR_BGR2GRAY)

# Apply edge detection
edges = cv2.Canny(gray_image, 100, 200)

# Display the images
plt.figure(figsize=(12, 6))
plt.subplot(1, 2, 1)
plt.imshow(cv2.cvtColor(gray_image, cv2.COLOR_BGR2RGB))
plt.title('Grayscale Image')
plt.subplot(1, 2, 2)
plt.imshow(cv2.cvtColor(edges, cv2.COLOR_BGR2RGB))
plt.title('Edge Detection')
plt.show()
```

In the above script,

- The script loads an image using OpenCV (cv2.imread).
- The image is converted to grayscale, which is a common preprocessing step.
- Edge detection is applied to the grayscale image using the Canny algorithm, highlighting the edges in the image.
- The original grayscale and edge-detected images are displayed using Matplotlib.

This above sample program demonstrates transforming of images to extract useful information or features. These techniques lay the groundwork for more advanced computer vision tasks, such as object recognition, scene understanding, and image classification.

Using CNN for Image Processing

Convolutional Neural Networks (CNNs) offer a more advanced approach to image processing, especially when dealing with tasks that require understanding the content of the image, such as classification, object detection, or segmentation. CNNs are especially adept at automatically learning and extracting features from images, which is a significant leap from traditional image processing techniques.

In a typical CNN architecture for image processing, the network learns to identify various features of the image through its layers, starting from simple edges and textures in the initial layers to more complex patterns in the deeper layers. This process makes CNNs incredibly powerful for complex image understanding tasks.

We will create a simple CNN model and demonstrate its application using a sample image. For this practical walkthrough, we will use a pre-trained CNN model from Keras called VGG16, which is widely used for image classification tasks.

First, ensure you have the necessary libraries installed:

```
pip install tensorflow
```

For the practical demonstration, you'll need a sample image. This image can be any standard image file (like JPEG or PNG). You can use an image from a dataset, a stock photo, or even take a picture yourself. Just ensure it's representative of the kind of images the VGG16 model was trained on (e.g., objects, animals, scenes).

And then proceed with the following script:

```
import numpy as np
import matplotlib.pyplot as plt
from tensorflow.keras.applications.vgg16 import VGG16, preprocess_input,
decode_predictions
from tensorflow.keras.preprocessing import image

# Load VGG16 pre-trained model
model = VGG16(weights='imagenet')

# Load a sample image and preprocess it
img_path = 'path_to_sample_image.jpg'  # Replace with your image path
```

```
img = image.load_img(img_path, target_size=(224, 224))  # Resize image
x = image.img_to_array(img)
x = np.expand_dims(x, axis=0)
x = preprocess_input(x)

# Predict the class of the image
predictions = model.predict(x)
predicted_class = decode_predictions(predictions, top=1)[0][0][1]

# Display the image and prediction
plt.imshow(img)
plt.title(f'Predicted Class: {predicted_class}')
plt.show()
```

In the above script,

- We use the VGG16 model pre-trained on ImageNet, a large dataset of labeled images.
- The sample image is loaded and preprocessed to fit the input requirements of VGG16 (resizing to 224x224 and applying specific preprocessing steps).
- The model makes a prediction on the image, which we decode into a human-readable class.
- Finally, we display the image along with the predicted class.

The above sample program demonstrates how CNNs, especially pre-trained models, can be leveraged for sophisticated image processing tasks, surpassing traditional methods in their ability to understand and interpret the content of images.

Summary

This chapter takes you on a tour through the intertwined worlds of Natural Language Processing (NLP) and Computer Vision (CV), two critical AI domains that are reshaping our interactions with technology. We delved into the complexities of text processing in the NLP segment, beginning with fundamental concepts like tokenization and vectorization. We investigated various vectorization techniques, such as one-hot encoding, Bag of Words, n-grams, and TF-IDF, each of which plays a distinct role in converting textual data into numerical formats. Our understanding was further enhanced by the advanced leap into word embeddings, where we saw how models like GloVe encapsulate semantic relationships in dense vector spaces. This shift from simple word representations to nuanced, context-aware embeddings highlighted the depth and complexity of NLP.

The hands-on experience with these concepts was provided by the practical demonstrations throughout the NLP section, particularly using our simulated coffee preferences dataset. To break down text, we used tokenization, then BoW and TF-IDF for basic text analysis before moving on to pre-trained GloVe embeddings for deeper text interpretation. This progression from basic text processing to the use of sophisticated embedding techniques demonstrated the evolution of NLP by demonstrating its ability to extract rich, meaningful insights from language.

Switching gears to Computer Vision, the chapter laid the groundwork for understanding how computers interpret visual data by introducing the fundamental principles of image processing. We looked at image processing techniques like edge detection and color space transformations, laying the groundwork for more complex CV tasks. The conversation then moved on to the topics of object detection and face recognition, two of the most dynamic and influential areas of CV. We investigated the architecture and functionality of game-changing models such as YOLO for object detection and FaceNet for face recognition, demonstrating how these models have transformed the field. These sections illuminated not only the technical aspects of CV, but also its diverse applications, which ranged from autonomous driving and medical imaging to security and personal authentication.

The balance between theoretical understanding and practical application was maintained throughout the chapter, ensuring a comprehensive learning experience. This chapter's exploration of NLP and CV painted a vivid picture of how AI is more than just a computational tool; it is a transformative force in interpreting and understanding both text and visual data, opening up new frontiers in human-computer interaction.

CHAPTER 7: HANDS-ON REINFORCEMENT LEARNING

Introduction

Sequential Decision Making

Sequential decision making is a complex and dynamic process that is important in a variety of fields, ranging from strategic games like chess to advanced fields like reinforcement learning (RL) and artificial intelligence. This process is distinguished by a series of interconnected decisions made over time, each of which has the potential to significantly influence future outcomes and the overall goal. Sequential decision making in broader contexts requires a similar depth of strategy and foresight as chess players consider each move carefully, considering not only the immediate impact but also the longer-term implications on the game.

Sequential decision making is central to agent behavior in the realm of RL. In this context, an agent is an entity that interacts with its environment, making decisions or taking actions based on its current state at each step. The agent's ultimate goal is to maximize some concept of cumulative reward over time. This cumulative reward is a comprehensive measure that includes the long-term effects and benefits of the actions taken, rather than just a sum of immediate returns.

The complexities of sequential decision making in RL can be seen through the lens of a learning process, in which the agent gradually refines its decision-making strategy through repeated interactions with the environment. This is typically accomplished through trial and error, a method that allows the agent to experiment with various actions and understand the consequences of those actions. Over time, the agent develops a policy, which is a set of rules or a strategy that dictates the best action to take in each state in order to maximize its cumulative reward.

Key Components of Sequential Decision Making

Agent

The agent, the entity that learns from and makes decisions within its environment, is at the heart of RL. The agent's role is similar to that of a learner or decision-maker. It monitors the environment, acts, and receives feedback in the form of rewards or penalties. The agent continuously learns from these interactions, refining its decision-making strategy to more effectively achieve its goals.

The environment includes everything with which the agent interacts. It is an external entity that displays states to the agent and provides feedback on the agent's actions. The environment is dynamic, and it can change in response to the actions of the agent, presenting new scenarios and challenges. The complexity and unpredictability of the environment influence the agent's learning process and strategy.

State

A state is a particular representation or snapshot of the environment at a specific point in time. It gives the agent the information he or she needs about the current situation or condition of the environment. The state is what the agent observes and relies on to make decisions. The quality and quantity of information available in the state can have a significant impact on the agent's decision-making process.

Actions

The choices or moves that the agent can make in response to the state of the environment are referred to as actions. The agent's action space is the collection of all possible actions available to it. The nature and range of available actions can vary greatly depending on the specific problem and environment with which the agent is dealing. The ability of the agent to choose the appropriate action in a given state is critical to its success.

Rewards

The environment communicates the consequences of the agent's actions through the feedback mechanism of rewards. They can be positive (encouraging desirable behavior) or negative (discouraging undesirable behavior). The agent's learning process is supervised by the reward system, which incentivizes it to make decisions that maximize cumulative rewards over time.

Policy

The policy is the strategy or rule-set that the agent uses to determine its actions based on the current state. It essentially maps states to actions and is a critical component in determining the agent's behavior. A well-defined policy enables the agent to make decisions that are consistent and effective.

Value Function

The value function is an important concept in RL because it estimates how beneficial it is for the agent to be in a given state while taking into account potential future rewards. It aids in evaluating and comparing the desirability of various states, directing the agent toward states that are likely to yield higher long-term returns.

Environment Model

Some RL approaches include an environment model, which is an abstract representation that predicts how the environment will respond to certain actions. This model can be used to simulate the consequences of actions before they are carried out in the real world, allowing the agent to plan and make better decisions. Depending on the requirements of the RL problem and the availability of data about the environment, models can range from simple approximations to complex simulations.

In practical RL problems, sequential decision making is crucial. For example, in a game-playing AI, the agent needs to decide which moves to make at each step, considering not just immediate points but also setting up for future advantageous positions. In robotics, an RL agent might need to decide how to move to navigate effectively, considering both the immediate path and the ultimate goal.

Sequential decision making in RL involves learning the best actions to take in various states, often in complex environments with uncertain outcomes. The agent learns from experience, understanding the consequences of actions over time, which is a fundamental shift from the supervised learning paradigm where learning is from labeled data. As we progress through this chapter, we will explore how RL algorithms enable agents to learn effective decision-making strategies through interaction with their environment, making RL a powerful tool for solving a wide range of problems that require a series of decisions.

Action Values and Estimation Algorithm

Action Values

Action values, often denoted as Q-values, represent the expected utility (or total expected reward) of taking a certain action in a given state and following a specific policy thereafter. In simpler terms, it's a measure of how good it is for the agent to perform a particular action in a specific state.

The primary purpose of calculating action values is to guide the agent in choosing the action that maximizes the cumulative reward. The action with the highest Q-value for a particular state is considered the best action.

Estimation Algorithms for Action Values

Estimating action values is a fundamental task in RL, and several algorithms have been developed for this purpose. These can be broadly categorized into model-based and model-free methods:

Model-Based Methods

These methods involve creating a model of the environment which predicts the next state and reward for each action. The agent uses this model to estimate action values.

Example: Dynamic Programming methods like Value Iteration and Policy Iteration.

Model-Free Methods

In contrast, model-free methods do not require a model of the environment. They learn action values based on the experience of interacting with the environment.

Examples: Temporal Difference (TD) Learning, Q-Learning, and SARSA (State-Action-Reward-State-Action).

Q-Learning

Q-Learning is an off-policy TD learning algorithm. It estimates the value of the optimal policy, regardless of the agent's actions, by learning the optimal Q-values for each state-action pair.

The agent updates its Q-values using the formula:

$$Q(s,a)=Q(s,a)+\alpha[r+\gamma \max_{a'} Q(s',a')-Q(s,a)]$$

where,

- α is the learning rate,
- γ is the discount factor,
- s is the current state,
- a is the current action,
- r is the reward, and
- s is the new state.

The key idea is to update the Q-value of the current state-action pair toward the reward plus the highest Q-value of the next state. Q-Learning can handle problems with stochastic transitions and rewards without requiring a model of the environment. It is suitable for learning optimal policies in Markov Decision Processes (MDPs).

Implementing Q-Learning typically involves initializing a Q-table, exploring the environment, and updating the Q-values based on the experiences. This approach allows the agent to gradually learn the best actions to take in different states, leading to the discovery of optimal policies.

Markov Decision Process (MDP)

Transitioning to Markov Decision Processes (MDP), we're now entering a key conceptual area in Reinforcement Learning. An MDP provides a mathematical framework for modeling decision-making situations where outcomes are partly random and partly under the control of a decision-maker. Let us first understand how to translate a problem into an MDP and then create an MDP for our coffee app example.

Translating a Problem into MDP

Identifying Components of an MDP

To frame a problem as an MDP, you need to identify its key components: states (S), actions (A), transition probabilities (P), rewards (R), and possibly a discount factor (γ).

States (S)

Determine what constitutes a 'state' in your problem. States should capture all relevant information from which the agent makes decisions.

Actions (A)

Define the set of actions available to the agent in each state. Actions are the choices the agent can make.

Transition Probabilities (P)

Establish the probability of moving from one state to another, given an action. This is often where the stochastic nature of the problem comes in.

Rewards (R)

Specify the reward received after transitions from one state to another due to an action. Rewards direct the agent towards desirable states.

Discount Factor (γ)

Decide on a discount factor that defines the present value of future rewards, reflecting the trade-off between immediate and future rewards.

Sample Program: Creating an MDP

We will consider our coffee app scenario and frame it as an MDP, wherein the following can be defined:

- States (S): States could represent different customer profiles or situations. For instance, a state might encapsulate a customer's previous coffee choices, the time of day, and the customer's rating history.

- Actions (A):Actions might include recommending a specific type of coffee to a customer or perhaps offering a discount on a certain product.

- Transition Probabilities (P): These would be the probabilities of a customer transitioning from one state to another, based on the action taken. For example, if we recommend an Espresso, what's the probability that the customer's next choice will be a Latte?

- Rewards (R): Rewards could be defined in terms of customer satisfaction or sales. For instance, a positive customer review or increased sales of a recommended coffee type could yield a higher reward.

- Discount Factor (γ): If long-term customer engagement is more valuable than immediate sales, a higher discount factor could be used to prioritize future rewards.

An MDP often involves gathering data about the states, actions, transitions, and rewards, and for our coffee app, this would mean collecting and analyzing customer data to understand their preferences and behaviors, and then using this data to estimate the MDP components. After framing an MDP, we can apply RL algorithms to learn optimal policies for actions like personalized coffee recommendations.

Rewards and Tasks

Overview

In RL, a reward is a signal sent from the environment to the agent after it takes an action. It's a numerical value that indicates the benefit (or cost) of the action taken by the agent in a given state. The reward mechanism directs the learning process of the agent. By receiving rewards or penalties, the agent learns which actions are beneficial and should be repeated, and which should be avoided.

The goal of an RL agent is often to maximize cumulative rewards over time, not just immediate rewards. This introduces the concept of long-term vs. short-term rewards and the trade-offs between them.

Michael Littman's Hypothesis on Reward

Michael Littman, a prominent figure in RL, has provided valuable insights into how rewards can be structured and their impact on the learning process. Littman's work emphasizes "reward shaping," a method to accelerate learning by providing additional rewards or penalties. It involves modifying the standard reward structure to make the learning process faster and more efficient.

One of Littman's key hypotheses is about balancing immediate and long-term rewards. The hypothesis suggests that providing too much emphasis on immediate rewards can lead to suboptimal long-term strategies. Littman also posits that the reward function should accurately reflect the desired behavior. Misalignment between the reward structure and the intended objective can lead the agent to learn undesired behaviors.

In the context of our coffee app MDP, the rewards could be structured to reflect customer satisfaction or sales. For example, positive feedback or repeat purchases might yield higher rewards. Following Littman's hypothesis, it's important to ensure that the rewards not only incentivize immediate sales but also promote long-term customer engagement and satisfaction.
Reward Shaping for Effective Learning: We might implement reward shaping by providing additional rewards for actions that lead to new customer acquisition or retaining loyal customers, thus accelerating the learning of beneficial behaviors. This approach underscores the significance of Littman's insights in designing effective RL solutions, where the reward structure is a critical determinant of the agent's learning and success.

Continuing Tasks

Continuing tasks are scenarios where the interaction between the agent and the environment goes on indefinitely, without a natural endpoint. These tasks are ongoing, and the agent continually makes decisions and receives feedback. These tasks often involve a continuous stream of decisions and rewards. They require the agent to balance long-term strategies against immediate rewards effectively.

For example, imagine an RL agent tasked with maintaining continuous engagement with customers through the coffee app. The agent's decisions could involve timely coffee recommendations, promotional offers, or feedback requests, with the goal of keeping customers engaged over an extended period without a specific ending.

Episodic Tasks

Episodic tasks involve interactions that break down into distinct episodes. Each episode has a clear start and end, and the agent's goal is often to maximize its reward within each episode. After each episode, the environment resets to a standard starting state or a new state for the next episode. These tasks are suitable for learning situations where the agent's actions lead to a definite outcome, after which the scenario restarts.

For example, consider an episodic task where each episode is a customer's order process, from order placement to completion. The RL agent could make decisions to optimize order handling, such as predicting and preparing for upcoming orders based on current trends. Once an order is completed (the episode ends), the system resets to handle the next order.

The distinction between these two types of tasks is crucial for designing the right RL approach. The main difference lies in how the agent's interaction with the environment is temporally structured. Continuing tasks are like a never-ending story, while episodic tasks are akin to chapters in a book, each with a clear beginning and end. In continuing tasks, the agent must focus more on long-term strategies due to the ongoing nature of the task. In contrast, in episodic tasks, the agent focuses on achieving the best outcome within the finite scope of an episode.

In our coffee app example, recognizing whether a task is continuing or episodic helps in structuring the reward system and defining the agent's objectives appropriately. It directs the design of the RL model, ensuring that the agent's learning and decision-making processes align with the specific dynamics of each task.

Reinforcement Learning Policies

Concept of Policy

A policy in RL is a strategy used by the agent to decide its actions in each state. Essentially, it's a rule or a set of rules that dictates the course of action an agent should take when in a specific state. Policies are central in RL as they drive the agent's decision-making process. The goal of most RL problems is to learn an optimal policy that maximizes the expected reward over time. Policies allow an agent to adapt its behavior based on the state it's in, making RL suitable for complex, dynamic environments.

There are two types of policies such as deterministic policy and stochastic policy. In deterministic policy, a specific action is chosen for each state. It's a direct mapping from states to actions. Whereas, the stochastic policy involves some level of randomness. Instead of a specific action, probabilities are assigned to each action in a state, indicating the likelihood of taking each action.

Specifying Policies

Specifying a Deterministic Policy

This can be as simple as a lookup table or a function that maps each state to an action. For example, a deterministic policy could be a set rule like "If a customer frequently orders lattes in the morning, recommend a latte discount in the morning." A deterministic policy might always offer the same type of reward or recommendation under specific conditions.

Specifying a Stochastic Policy

Stochastic policies are often represented using probability distributions. For example, a stochastic policy might say, "If a customer orders espresso after 2 PM, there is a 70% chance of recommending a new espresso product and a 30% chance of recommending a related accessory." A stochastic policy might vary the recommendations, adding an element of exploration and potentially discovering more effective strategies to enhance customer satisfaction.

Policies are the guiding strategies behind an agent's actions and learning process in RL. In the next section, we will explore how these policies can be evaluated and improved upon, leading towards the development of optimal strategies for complex decision-making tasks like those in our coffee app example.

Values and Bellman Equation

What are Value Functions?

Value functions are critical in RL as they provide a measure of how good it is for an agent to be in a given state (state-value function) or how good it is to perform a certain action in a state (action-value function). Value functions help the agent in evaluating how beneficial different states or actions are, aiding in decision-making and policy improvement.

There are two primary types of value functions:

- State-Value Function (V): Gives the expected return (cumulative discounted rewards) starting from a state s and following policy π.
- Action-Value Function (Q): Provides the expected return starting from state s, taking an action a, and thereafter following policy π.

The Bellman Equation

The Bellman equation, formulated by Richard Bellman, is a fundamental recursive relationship used in dynamic programming and RL. It breaks down the value functions into components that are easier to compute and understand. It expresses the relationship between the value of a state and the values of its successor states.

Forms of the Bellman Equation:

For the state-value function:

$$V(s)=\sum a\ \pi(a|s)\sum s',r\ P(s',r|s,a)[r+\gamma V(s')]$$

For the action-value function:

$$Q(s,a)=\sum s',r\ P(s',r|s,a)[r+\gamma\sum a'\ \pi(a'|s')Q(s',a')]$$

Here, γ is the discount factor, π is the policy, and P is the transition probability.

In our coffee app example, we could estimate the expected future satisfaction of a customer based on the current state (e.g., recent purchase history, time of day). We might evaluate the expected satisfaction from recommending a specific coffee or promotion. We could also use the Bellman equation to iteratively update the value estimates. For example, updating the value of recommending a particular coffee type based on customer feedback and the expected long-term customer engagement.

Dynamic Programming (DP)

What is DP?

Dynamic programming is a method for solving complex problems by breaking them down into simpler subproblems and solving each of these subproblems just once, storing their solutions. In the context of RL, DP is used to compute value functions and find optimal policies when the model of the environment (i.e., the transition probabilities and rewards) is known.

Following are the key principles of DP in RL:

- Optimal Substructure: The principle that optimal solutions of subproblems can be used to find the optimal solution of the overall problem.
- Overlapping Subproblems: Many subproblems recur in the process, and DP saves their solutions in a table to avoid redundant calculations.

Dynamic Programming Algorithms

Policy Evaluation

This is used to compute the value function for a given policy. The algorithm iteratively applies the Bellman Expectation Equation until the value function converges.

Policy Iteration

This involves two steps: policy evaluation and policy improvement. The algorithm evaluates a policy, then improves it by making it greedy with respect to the value function. This process repeats until the policy is optimal.

Value Iteration

Value iteration combines the policy evaluation and improvement steps. It iteratively updates the value function and the policy until it converges to the optimal policy.

Sample Program: Policy Evaluation

We will demonstrate policy evaluation considering we have a simplified version of our coffee app MDP and want to evaluate a given policy.

For simplicity, we will assume:

- There are three states: A, B, and C, representing different customer interactions.
- The agent has two actions in each state: action 1 (recommend coffee) and action 2 (offer discount).
- The rewards and transition probabilities are known.

Following is a simple and easy python implementation:

```
import numpy as np


# Assume a simple MDP with 3 states and transition probabilities and rewards
transition_probabilities = {
```

```
    'A': {'a1': {'A': 0.8, 'B': 0.2}, 'a2': {'A': 0.7, 'C': 0.3}},
    'B': {'a1': {'B': 0.9, 'C': 0.1}, 'a2': {'B': 0.4, 'A': 0.6}},
    'C': {'a1': {'C': 1.0}, 'a2': {'C': 1.0}}
}
rewards = {'A': 1, 'B': 2, 'C': 0}

# Assume a given policy
policy = {'A': 'a1', 'B': 'a1', 'C': 'a2'}

# Initialize value function to zero
V = {'A': 0, 'B': 0, 'C': 0}
gamma = 0.9  # discount factor

# Policy evaluation loop
for _ in range(100):  # Assuming 100 iterations for convergence
    for state in V:
        action = policy[state]
        V[state] = sum([transition_probabilities[state][action][next_state] *
                        (rewards[next_state] + gamma * V[next_state])
                        for next_state in transition_probabilities[state][action]])

print("Value function:", V)
```

In the above script,

- We define a simple MDP with states, actions, transition probabilities, and rewards.
- A policy is specified where certain actions are chosen in each state.
- The value function for each state is calculated based on the policy and the Bellman Expectation Equation.

The assessment of states, actions, and probabilities would be much more extensive, and computational techniques like iterative or approximate methods would be necessary. The core principles remain the same: breaking down the problem, using the Bellman equation, and iteratively refining the value function to evaluate or improve a policy. This process is central to finding optimal strategies in RL.

Constructing Algorithm

Value Iteration Algorithm Overview

Value Iteration is a method of computing the optimal policy and the optimal value function in a Markov Decision Process (MDP). It iteratively updates the value function for each state and then derives the policy that maximizes the expected reward.

Value Iteration Key Steps

- Initialization: Start with an arbitrary value function, typically initialized to zero.
- Iteration: For each state, update the value function based on the maximum expected return achievable, considering all possible actions.
- Policy Extraction: Once the value function converges, extract the policy that maximizes the expected reward given this value function.

Sample Program: Implement Value Iteration

Let us consider we have a simplified MDP as below:

- States: Different customer profiles based on their purchase history.
- Actions: Two actions - "Recommend Coffee" and "Offer Discount".
- Rewards: Based on customer satisfaction or sales increase.
- Transition Probabilities: Chances of moving from one customer profile to another based on actions.

We then implement Value Iteration in the below sample program:

```
import numpy as np

# Define states, actions, rewards, and transition probabilities
states = ['Profile1', 'Profile2', 'Profile3']
actions = ['Recommend', 'Discount']
rewards = {'Profile1': 2, 'Profile2': 5, 'Profile3': 1}
```

```
transition_probabilities = {
    'Profile1': {'Recommend': {'Profile2': 0.7, 'Profile3': 0.3},
              'Discount': {'Profile1': 0.6, 'Profile2': 0.4}},
    'Profile2': {'Recommend': {'Profile3': 0.5, 'Profile1': 0.5},
              'Discount': {'Profile2': 0.8, 'Profile3': 0.2}},
    'Profile3': {'Recommend': {'Profile1': 0.4, 'Profile2': 0.6},
              'Discount': {'Profile3': 1.0}}
}
gamma = 0.9  # Discount factor

# Initialize value function
V = np.zeros(len(states))

# Value iteration algorithm
for _ in range(100):  # Run for 100 iterations
    V_prev = np.copy(V)
    for i, state in enumerate(states):
        V[i] = max([sum([transition_probabilities[state][action][next_state] *
                    (rewards[next_state] + gamma * V_prev[list(states).index(next_state)])
                    for next_state in transition_probabilities[state][action]])
                for action in actions])

# Extract policy from value function
policy = {}
for i, state in enumerate(states):
    policy[state] =
actions[np.argmax([sum([transition_probabilities[state][action][next_state] *
                                    (rewards[next_state] + gamma *
V[list(states).index(next_state)])
```

```
                for next_state in transition_probabilities[state][action]])
            for action in actions])]

print("Optimal Value Function:", V)
print("Optimal Policy:", policy)
```

In the above script,

- We defined a simple representation of our coffee app scenario with states, actions, rewards, and transition probabilities.
- The Value Iteration algorithm iteratively updates the value function for each state.
- After the value function converges, we extract the optimal policy from it.

In each iteration, the algorithm updates the value of each state by considering the best action that maximizes the expected reward. Based on the final value function, we determine the best action for each state, forming the optimal policy. The optimal policy derived represents the best action (either recommending a coffee or offering a discount) for each customer profile to maximize overall customer satisfaction and sales.

Summary

This chapter introduced us to the complex world of sequential decision-making, where agents learn to make a series of decisions to achieve their goals. We began by deconstructing the concept of sequential decision making in reinforcement learning (RL), gaining a better understanding of how agents interact with their surroundings, make decisions, and learn from the outcomes of their actions. This interaction was framed within the context of Markov Decision Processes (MDPs), where we dissected the components necessary for modeling decision making problems, such as states, actions, rewards, and policies.

We delved deeper into the critical aspect of RL - policies and value functions. Policies, which define the agent's actions in each state, were investigated in both deterministic and stochastic forms. We saw how the agent's policy has a direct impact on its ability to achieve its objectives. We used value functions to estimate how good it is to be in a certain state or to take a specific action in order to quantify the quality of these policies. The introduction of the Bellman equation solidified our understanding by revealing how current decisions affect future rewards, an important concept in RL.

Dynamic programming techniques such as policy evaluation, policy iteration, and value iteration were used to put these concepts into practice. These methods provided a framework for improving the agent's policy in a systematic manner. We put these techniques into practice by modeling customer interactions with a simplified MDP in our coffee app scenario. We demonstrated how an RL agent could learn to recommend the optimal actions (such as coffee recommendations or discounts) to maximize customer satisfaction and sales by iterating over policies and updating value functions.

Finally, using the Value Iteration method, we built an algorithm that maximizes reward, providing a practical demonstration of how to calculate value functions and derive optimal policies. This application in our coffee app example demonstrated how RL can be used to solve real-world problems in which an agent must make a series of decisions in an uncertain environment.

The seamless integration of theoretical concepts with practical walkthrough throughout the chapter provided a thorough understanding of RL's core principles. This in-depth look at sequential decision-making, policy formulation, and the pursuit of optimal strategies in RL shed light on how agents learn to navigate complex environments, making intelligent decisions that add up to achieve long-term goals.

CHAPTER 8: ETHICS TO AI

Ethics in Technology

Ethics in technology refers to the moral principles that govern the behavior and decision-making processes in the development, deployment, and use of technological products and services. It's about asking not just "Can we?" but "Should we?" Imagine you're building a bridge. You'd want it to be not only strong and durable but also safe for everyone. Similarly, when we develop technology, especially something as influential as AI, we need to ensure it's not only effective and efficient but also fair, safe, and beneficial for society.

As AI becomes more integrated into our daily lives, the ethical implications are too significant to ignore.

Developers and Designers

- Ethical Design: As someone creating AI, imagine you're setting the rules for how this AI will interact with the world. It's crucial to embed ethical considerations right from the design stage.
- Bias Mitigation: Being aware of and actively working to reduce biases in AI models is essential. This includes ensuring diverse datasets and being mindful of the model's potential limitations.

Businesses and Organizations

- Ethical Deployment: For businesses deploying AI solutions, it's about using AI responsibly. This means considering the broader impact of AI decisions on customers, employees, and society.
- Regulatory Compliance: Following legal and ethical standards, and staying updated with evolving regulations around AI.

End-Users and Society

- Awareness and Advocacy: As users, staying informed about how AI impacts us and advocating for ethical AI practices is key. It's about having a say in how this technology shapes our world.
- Participatory Approach: Encouraging a participatory approach in AI development, where diverse voices and perspectives are included, can lead to more ethically aligned AI systems.

Just like AI as any member in a community, it should contribute positively, respect others' rights, and be held accountable for its actions. This is where ethics transforms from a concept into a guiding principle for action. Whether you're developing AI, using AI-based services, or simply impacted by AI decisions, understanding and contributing to this dialogue is crucial. It's about shaping technology in a way that aligns with our values and aspirations as a society.

As we progress through this chapter, we will discuss frameworks and guidelines, Responsible AI and Trustworthy AI that are being developed to steer AI towards a more ethical and beneficial path.

AI Ethical Framework (EAAI)

The American Council for Technology-Industry Advisory Council (ACT-IAC) is a non-profit educational organization focused on enhancing government mission outcomes through collaboration, leadership, and education. It serves as an objective and trusted forum where government and industry executives collaborate to improve public services and agency operations through technology. ACT-IAC emphasizes communication, innovative problem-solving, and workforce development, contributing to better government-industry relations and outcomes. This organization also facilitates the participation of all public and private organizations committed to improving public services through effective technology use.

The ACT-IAC developed an ethical framework for AI called the Ethical Application of Artificial Intelligence Framework (EAAI). It provides a comprehensive structure for assessing the ethical implications of AI. It focuses on five core components:

1. Bias: Examines biases in AI systems and data. The framework guides evaluating and mitigating biases to ensure equitable AI outcomes.

2. Fairness: Addresses fairness in AI applications. It provides methods for assessing and promoting fairness in AI decisions and impacts.

3. Transparency: Emphasizes the importance of transparent AI processes and decisions. The framework offers strategies for enhancing AI transparency, making it understandable and auditable.

4. Responsibility: Focuses on the responsible development and use of AI. It includes guidelines for ethical AI deployment, considering legality and societal impact.

5. Interpretability: Stresses the need for AI systems to be interpretable and understandable. The framework suggests approaches to improve the clarity of AI decision-making processes.

Following is a detailed exploration of each of the components of this framework:

Bias

Definition

Bias in AI refers to a systemic and non-random error that can lead to unfair outcomes. It often arises from the data used to train AI systems, which might be unrepresentative or prejudiced based on historical or societal inequalities.

Indicators

- Data Diversity: Ensuring a diverse range of data sources and types is used to prevent the over-representation of certain groups.
- Algorithmic Transparency: Understanding how algorithms make decisions and identifying points where bias could be introduced.
- Statistical Distribution: Monitoring for skewed data that could lead to biased outcomes.

Implications

- Unfair Treatment: Bias in AI can lead to unfair treatment of certain groups, reinforcing existing societal inequalities.
- Loss of Trust: Perceived or real biases in AI systems can erode trust among users and stakeholders.
- Legal and Ethical Challenges: Biased AI systems can lead to legal ramifications and ethical dilemmas, particularly when they affect decisions in critical areas like healthcare, finance, or law enforcement.

Monitor and Measure

- Regular Audits: Conducting regular audits of AI systems for bias, using both automated tools and human oversight.
- Feedback Loops: Implementing feedback mechanisms to identify and correct bias in AI systems continually.
- Impact Assessment: Evaluating the real-world impacts of AI systems to understand how they affect different groups.
- Model Validation: Ensuring that AI models are rigorously tested and validated against diverse datasets to minimize bias.

The Framework's approach to bias provides a holistic view, considering not just the technical aspects but also the broader social and ethical implications.

Fairness

Definition

Fairness in AI refers to the equitable and just treatment of all individuals by AI systems. It's about ensuring that AI decisions do not create or perpetuate discrimination or prejudice against any group or individual.

Indicators

- Equitable Outcomes: Assessing whether the AI system's decisions are equitable across different groups, especially marginalized or historically disadvantaged populations.

- Representation in Data: Ensuring that the data used for training AI systems fairly represents all relevant groups and demographics.
- Inclusivity in Design: Involving diverse stakeholders in the AI design process to understand and address various needs and perspectives.

Implications

- Social Impact: Unfair AI systems can exacerbate social inequalities and discrimination, impacting the lives and rights of individuals, particularly those in vulnerable groups.
- Legal Compliance: Many jurisdictions are implementing laws and regulations to ensure fairness in AI, making compliance a legal imperative.
- Public Trust: Fairness is crucial for maintaining public trust in AI technologies. Perceptions of unfairness can lead to a backlash against AI deployments.

Monitor and Measure

- Fairness Audits: Regularly conducting fairness audits to assess the impact of AI decisions across different groups.
- Algorithmic Impact Assessments: Evaluating the potential and actual impacts of AI algorithms on fairness, including unintended consequences.
- Transparency Reports: Publishing transparency reports that detail the efforts taken to ensure fairness and the findings from fairness assessments.

The Fairness component highlights the need for AI systems to be designed, developed, and deployed with a keen focus on equitable treatment involving careful consideration from the initial stages of data collection and model development to the final deployment and monitoring stages.

Transparency

Definition

Transparency in AI refers to the openness about the purpose, structure, and underlying actions of AI algorithms. It's about understanding how and why an AI system arrives at a given outcome, making AI explainable to users, decision-makers, and those impacted by AI.

Indicators

- Open Data Architecture and Algorithms: AI systems should employ open architecture and non-proprietary algorithms, enhancing transparency. When results can be tracked back from data architecture and algorithmic perspectives, it helps in understanding the AI decision-making process.
- Observable Systems: AI systems that are observable provide access to relevant information, resulting in explainability. This includes explaining the internal mechanics of AI in human terms.

- Explainability vs. Interpretability: While interpretability is about observing cause and effect within a system, explainability is about predicting what will happen with a change in input or algorithmic parameters. It involves explaining the lifecycle of aggregation, assessment, and answers in AI processes.

Implications

- Risk of AI Gone Wild: If transparency is not achieved, there is a risk of unforeseen flaws and issues in AI systems.
- Credibility and Trust: Transparency is crucial for building user confidence in AI systems. Users should be able to understand how AI systems reach conclusions, addressing basic risks and concerns.

Monitor and Measure

- Continuous Monitoring: Regular testing for quality and compliance is essential. This includes user feedback implementation, data bias checking, and evaluating the AI system's impact.
- Smart Metrics and KPIs: Tracking smart metrics and Key Performance Indicators (KPIs) throughout the AI system's lifecycle helps in assessing transparency.

Through this component, AI systems become more accessible and understandable, fostering a more inclusive and informed usage of AI technology.

Responsibility

Definition

Responsibility in AI involves ensuring accountability for the application and use of AI technology, as well as the resulting impact and consequences due to outcomes. It focuses on the appropriateness of using AI in specific contexts and protecting stakeholders from outcomes that may not align with the intended mission.

Indicators

- Purpose: Ensuring that AI systems are used in accordance with their designed purpose in support of the mission.
- Privacy: Protecting the privacy of all stakeholders, ensuring that personally identifiable information (PII) is not compromised.
- Pedigree: Ensuring data veracity before consuming data for usage. It involves validating the source and completeness of the data.
- Provenance: Auditing the evolution and maturation of data and model structures to verify authenticity and changes.

Implications

- Applicability: Misuse of AI systems for purposes other than intended can lead to unknown and potentially harmful outcomes.
- Legality: Failure to maintain privacy can challenge the legal aspects of AI systems.
- Authenticity: Lack of authentic data can lead to misplaced confidence in outcomes, negatively impacting the mission.
- Auditability: Inability to audit AI systems, including changes to data and models, can make AI behavior unreliable.

Responsibility focuses on the AI's use and the safeguarding of outcomes against misuse or unintended consequences. It emphasizes the need for AI systems to be used ethically, legally, and in alignment with their intended purpose, ensuring that they contribute positively to their respective missions.

Interpretability

Definition

Interpretability in AI involves the ability to understand and present clear, understandable explanations for the decisions and outputs of AI systems. It ensures that AI technology produces consistent results that are reliable and trustworthy.

Indicators

- Causality/Influences: Understanding the relational dependencies and how they are interpreted in AI systems.
- Correlation/Effect: Determining how the culmination of analysis in AI produces specific results.
- Consequences/Impact: Understanding how AI insights influence and affect the environment and decisions.
- Consistency/Reliability: Assessing the predictability of AI outcomes to provide repeatable results given similar circumstances.

Implications

- Inferences/Associations: Identifying how AI results can be interpreted based on one's perspective.
- Implications/Answers: Understanding how AI outcomes influence current perceptions and decisions.
- Impacts/Actions: Recognizing how AI results inform and transform operational paradigms.
- Credibility/Confidence: Ensuring data assessments inform analysis that ascertains knowledge accurately and reliably.

Interpretability is essential for ensuring that AI applications are understood and used correctly. With this, AI technology can instill credibility and establish trust among users, making AI more accessible and effective in achieving its intended mission.

Responsible AI

As we go deep into the subject of ethics in Artificial Intelligence, a critical aspect that stands out is the concept of Responsible AI. This term encapsulates the ethical, transparent, and accountable use of AI technologies in a manner that benefits society while respecting user rights and ensuring fairness and safety.

In the digital age, AI technologies are integral to our lives, influencing everything from our shopping experiences to medical treatments. As such, the need for AI to be responsible is paramount to ensure its positive impact. The rapid evolution of AI technologies and their widespread applications have raised concerns regarding privacy, security, fairness, and transparency. Addressing these concerns is crucial for maintaining public trust and ensuring the sustainable development of AI technologies. Responsible AI is about developing and deploying AI systems in a way that upholds ethical principles, aligns with societal norms, and respects human values and rights. It's not just about the technology itself, but about how it's used, the decisions it makes, and its impact on people and society.

Pillars of Responsible AI

Ethics and Governance

AI must adhere to ethical principles, including respect for human rights, privacy, non-discrimination, and fairness. Governance structures should be in place to ensure these principles are upheld. Ethical AI development involves the consideration of societal values and norms, ensuring that AI decisions do not harm individuals or communities. This particular aspect has already been well understood in the previous section.

Transparency and Explainability

AI systems should be transparent and their decisions explainable. Stakeholders should understand how and why a particular AI decision was made. This involves making AI algorithms auditable and comprehensible, enabling users to understand the rationale behind AI-driven decisions.

Fairness and Non-discriminatio

AI systems should be designed to prevent bias and discrimination. This includes ensuring that AI algorithms treat all groups of people fairly and do not perpetuate or exacerbate inequalities. Fairness in AI requires rigorous testing and validation to identify and mitigate any form of bias in AI models.

Privacy and Security

AI systems must protect user privacy and ensure data security. This involves securing AI systems against unauthorized access and ensuring that personal data is not misused. Privacy considerations include compliance with data protection regulations and respecting user consent in data collection and usage.

Reliability and Safety

AI systems should be reliable and safe. They must function as intended, and their actions should not cause harm to users or the environment. This requires thorough testing and validation of AI systems in real-world scenarios to ensure their reliability and safety.

Accountability

There should be clear accountability for AI decisions. Organizations deploying AI must be responsible for the outcomes of their AI systems. This involves establishing clear lines of responsibility and mechanisms for redress in case AI systems cause harm or make erroneous decisions.

Impact of Responsible AI

- Businesses that adopt responsible AI practices are likely to build greater trust among their customers and stakeholders. This trust translates into brand value, customer loyalty, and a competitive advantage.

- As governments and international bodies introduce regulations around AI, compliance becomes crucial. Responsible AI practices help businesses navigate these regulations, reducing legal risks and potential liabilities.

- Responsible AI encourages businesses to innovate in a way that is sustainable and aligned with societal values. It opens avenues for new, ethically-aligned products and services.

- A commitment to responsible AI can attract talent who want to work for ethical and socially responsible organizations. It also helps in retaining employees who value ethical practices.

- By ensuring fairness and transparency, businesses can provide better customer experiences. This can lead to increased customer satisfaction and loyalty.

- In a market where many companies use AI, those that use it responsibly can differentiate themselves, appealing to increasingly ethically conscious consumers and partners.

Overall, Responsible AI is not just a compliance checklist; it's a strategic approach that integrates ethical principles into the core of business operations and AI deployments. As AI continues to shape various aspects of our lives, the emphasis on responsible AI will only grow stronger. Businesses that proactively adopt responsible AI practices are poised to lead in this new era, creating AI solutions that are not only innovative but also ethical, equitable, and aligned with the greater good of society. This approach will be crucial in shaping a future where AI is a force for positive change, enhancing human capabilities while respecting our values and rights.

Trustworthy AI

Understanding Concept

"Trustworthy AI" is a concept that has gained significant momentum in the discourse surrounding artificial intelligence. It encompasses a range of principles and practices aimed at ensuring AI systems are reliable, safe, and operate in a manner that engenders trust among users and stakeholders. Trustworthy AI refers to AI systems that are designed and operated in a manner that is ethically sound, transparent, and respects user rights and societal norms. It's about creating AI systems that are not only technically proficient but also socially and ethically responsible.

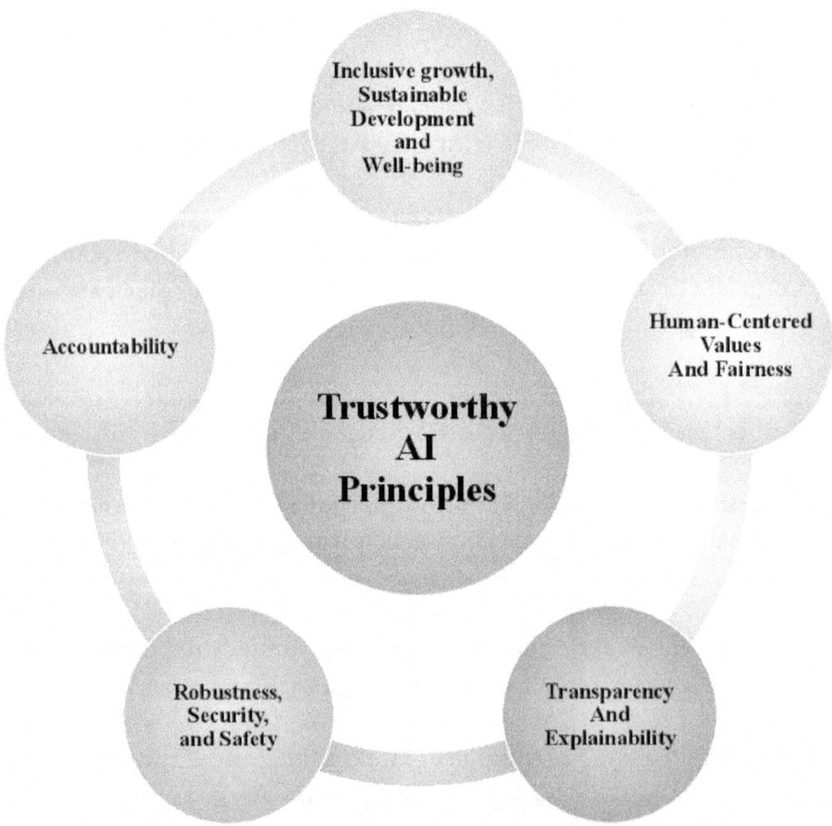

Fig 8.1 Principles of Trustworthy AI

Trustworthy AI is built on elements like transparency, reliability, fairness, safety, privacy, and accountability. It ensures that AI systems make decisions in a manner that is understandable and acceptable to humans.

Trustworthy AI vs. Responsible AI

While Trustworthy AI and Responsible AI are closely related and often overlap, there are subtle differences:

Responsible AI often focuses on the ethical development and deployment of AI technologies. It encompasses the broader responsibilities of organizations in using AI in ways that are ethical and beneficial to society. Trustworthy AI, on the other hand, centers more on the reliability and credibility of AI systems. It involves ensuring that AI systems are dependable and operate in a predictable and understandable manner.

Trustworthy AI places a stronger emphasis on the technical aspects of AI systems, including their safety, security, and robustness, ensuring they perform reliably under varied conditions.

Enabling Trustworthy AI

Audit and Assessment

Conduct comprehensive audits of existing AI systems to assess their compliance with Trustworthy AI principles. This includes evaluating algorithms for fairness, transparency, and bias.

Enhancing Data Integrity

Ensure the data used for training and operating AI systems is accurate, unbiased, and representative. Regularly update and cleanse data sets to maintain their integrity.

Implementing Explainable AI (XAI)

Adopt explainable AI practices to make the decision-making processes of AI systems transparent and understandable to users.

Continuous Testing and Validation

Regularly test AI systems for performance, safety, and reliability. Implement robust validation processes to ensure AI systems perform as expected in real-world scenarios.

Strengthening Security Measures

Enhance cybersecurity measures to protect AI systems from unauthorized access and manipulation. Ensure the security of both data and algorithms.

Establishing Ethical Governance

Set up governance frameworks to oversee the ethical implications of AI systems. This includes establishing ethical guidelines, oversight committees, and review processes.

Impact/Value for Businesses

Trustworthy AI can significantly enhance consumer trust in AI technologies. When consumers are confident that AI systems are reliable and ethical, they are more likely to adopt and interact positively with these technologies.The impact and value of Trustworthy AI for businesses are multifaceted and far-reaching as below:

Enhanced Consumer Trust and Adoption

Trustworthy AI plays a crucial role in building consumer confidence in AI technologies. When consumers believe that AI systems are reliable, ethical, and transparent, their willingness to adopt and engage with these technologies increases significantly. This trust fosters a positive relationship between consumers and AI-driven products or services, potentially leading to increased customer loyalty, higher satisfaction rates, and a broader consumer base.

Market Differentiation and Competitive Advantage

In industries where AI is a key component, prioritizing Trustworthy AI can serve as a powerful differentiator in the marketplace. Businesses that are known for their ethical AI practices and responsible use of AI can establish a unique position, setting themselves apart from competitors. This differentiation is increasingly important in a market where consumers and clients are becoming more aware of and concerned about the ethical implications of AI.

Compliance with Regulations and Reduced Risks

As AI technology evolves, so do the regulations and standards governing its use. Adhering to the principles of Trustworthy AI can help businesses stay ahead of these regulatory changes, ensuring compliance and minimizing legal and reputational risks. This proactive approach to regulation can prevent costly legal battles and protect the company's reputation in the long run.

Improved Decision-Making with Reliable Outputs

Trustworthy AI systems are designed to provide outputs that are not only accurate but also unbiased and fair. This leads to better, more informed decision-making within organizations. Reliable AI-driven insights can enhance various aspects of business operations, from strategic planning to customer service, ultimately contributing to improved performance and profitability.

Fostering Ethical Innovation

A commitment to Trustworthy AI encourages the development of AI solutions that are not just technologically advanced but also ethically sound and socially responsible. This approach ensures that AI technologies align with societal values and contribute positively to the community. It drives innovation in a direction that is sustainable and beneficial for both the business and society at large.

Attracting and Retaining Talent

Companies known for their dedication to ethical practices in AI are more likely to attract and retain top talent. Professionals, especially those in the tech industry, increasingly seek out employers who value responsible and ethical development of technology. By prioritizing Trustworthy AI, businesses can create a work environment that appeals to these values, attracting skilled professionals who are committed to ethical technology development.

Building Long-Term Sustainable Business Practices

Integrating Trustworthy AI principles into business operations contributes to the creation of sustainable, long-term business practices. It encourages a forward-thinking mindset, focusing on the future implications of AI technologies and their impact on various stakeholders. This long-term perspective is crucial for businesses aiming to thrive in an evolving technological landscape.

Enhancing Brand Reputation and Customer Loyalty

Trustworthy AI can significantly boost a company's brand reputation. When customers recognize a company's commitment to ethical AI, it can lead to increased loyalty and advocacy. This positive brand perception is invaluable in today's competitive business environment, where consumers are increasingly making choices based on corporate values and ethical considerations.

Investing in Trustworthy AI is a strategic decision for businesses that can lead to long-term success, consumer trust, and market leadership. In order to ensure that AI is used for everyone's benefit, Trustworthy AI is going to be more important as AI develops and becomes more integrated into different parts of society and businesses.

Summary

This chapter walked us through the critical role of ethics in the field of artificial intelligence, emphasizing the key elements that shape Trustworthy and Responsible AI. At its core, Trustworthy AI is concerned with developing AI systems that are not only technologically advanced but also reliable, ethical, and consistent with human values and societal norms. This concept is inextricably linked to Responsible AI, which focuses on the ethical development and deployment of AI, emphasizing organizations' broader responsibilities to use AI in ways that benefit and respect society.

We dissected Trustworthy AI's key elements, which included transparency, reliability, fairness, safety, privacy, and accountability. These components are essential for developing AI systems that are reliable and operate in a way that users can trust and understand. The distinction between Trustworthy and Responsible AI was clarified, emphasizing that, while both share common goals,

Trustworthy AI emphasizes the technical robustness and credibility of AI systems. Implementing Trustworthy AI entails conducting rigorous audits, improving data integrity, implementing explainable AI practices, conducting continuous testing and validation, strengthening security measures, and establishing ethical governance.

Trustworthy AI has a significant impact and value for businesses. Businesses that embrace these principles can increase consumer trust, gain a competitive advantage, ensure compliance with emerging regulations, improve decision-making, foster innovation, and attract top talent. In a market increasingly reliant on AI technologies, trustworthy AI not only serves as a moral compass but also as a strategic business advantage.

The discussion of ethics in AI in this chapter served as a timely reminder of the importance of incorporating ethical considerations into AI development. As AI becomes more integrated into our daily lives, a focus on responsible and trustworthy practices is critical for its long-term and beneficial growth. This journey through the ethical landscape of AI emphasized the role of technologists, businesses, and society in shaping a future in which AI is a force for good, enhancing human capabilities while upholding our values and rights.

Thank You

Index

Q

R

S

T

U

V

W

Epilogue

As we get to the end of our "Python AI Programming" trip, you will be on the verge of a new beginning, armed with the information and skills to explore the vast world of AI. This book was about more than just learning Python and comprehending AI algorithms; it was about imagining your place in the ever-changing story of artificial intelligence.

You've learned the fundamentals of Python, the mechanics of machine learning models, the depths of deep learning, and the complexity of NLP and computer vision. You've also navigated the ethical landscapes that govern artificial intelligence, ensuring that the technology you create is not just strong but also principled and responsible.

Remember that the end of this book does not mean the end of your education. It's a call to keep exploring, experimenting, and innovating. The world of AI is dynamic and ever-changing, and you are now a part of this fascinating evolution as a Python AI programmer.

Apply what you've learned to real-world challenges. Contribute to initiatives and research that push the limits of what AI is capable of. Collaborate with classmates, mentors, and the worldwide community to expand your knowledge and skills. Most importantly, apply your knowledge to make a good difference in business, science, healthcare, education, or any other industry where AI is used.

As you close this book, let your mind wander to the infinite possibilities. You are no longer just a reader or a student; you are an AI engineer, a creator, and a visionary. Go forth and contribute to the creation of a future in which AI and humanity coexist, powered by the power of Python and the inventiveness of brains like yours.

www.ingramcontent.com/pod-product-compliance
Lightning Source LLC
Chambersburg PA
CBHW080213170726
48282CB00030B/1107
* 9 7 8 8 1 1 9 1 7 7 6 3 9 *